The
MINIMALIST
Cooks at HOME

Mark Bittman

Recipes That

Give You

More Flavor

from *Fewer* Ingredients

in Less Time

The
MINIMALIST

Cooks at HOME

BROADWAY BOOKS | NEW YORK

BROADWAY

THE MINIMALIST COOKS AT HOME. Copyright © 2000, 2002 by Mark
Bittman. All rights reserved. Printed in the United States of
America. No part of this book may be reproduced or transmitted in
any form or by any means, electronic or mechanical, including
photocopying, recording, or by any information storage and
retrieval system, without written permission from the publisher.
For information, address Broadway Books, a division of Random
House, Inc., 1540 Broadway, New York, NY 10036.

Broadway Books titles may be purchased for business or
promotional use or for special sales. For information, please write
to: Special Markets Department, Random House, Inc., 1540
Broadway, New York, NY 10036.

BROADWAY BOOKS and its logo, a letter B bisected on the diagonal,
are trademarks of Broadway Books, a division of Random House, Inc.

Visit our Web site at www.broadwaybooks.com

Library of Congress has already cataloged a prior edition as follows:

Bittman, Mark.
    The minimalist cooks at home: recipes that give you more
    flavor from fewer ingredients in less time / Mark Bittman.—
    1st ed.
        p.   cm.
    Includes index.
    1. Cookery.   I. Title.
    TX718.B575   2000
    641.5—dc21   99-36291
                                                      CIP

ISBN 0-7679-0926-7

PRINTED IN UNITED STATES OF AMERICA

02 03 04 05 06 10 9 8 7 6 5 4 3 2 1

For Emma, Kate, Murray, and Gertrude

Acknowledgments

In 1995 Trish Hall, then editor of *The New York Times Living Section,* asked me to develop a weekly column. Two years later, when the section was relaunched as Dining In/Dining Out, that column became "The Minimalist." The column title, and indeed its theme, were the brainchildren of Rick Flaste, an inspired and inspiring editor and person. Though there are dozens of people I'm grateful to for their help and support in my work on the column and *The Minimalist Cooks at Home,* Trish and Rick are chief among them, and I'm happily in their debt for life.

My current editors at the *Times,* Michalene Busico, Pat Gurosky, and Roberta Zeff, are wonderful colleagues and brilliant word-and-idea people, who guide me in improving each column after I "finish" it. Regina Schrambling also worked on many of the columns that have made their way into this book.

Scores of chefs, fellow food-writers, and home cooks, especially in the New York area but all over the world, have given me great ideas for "the Mini"—trying to single them out would only offend those I miss. Thanks of course to Jennifer Josephy, my current editor at Broadway, and Harriet Bell, who edited the first edition of this book; to Bill Shinker, who first acquired this book, and Steve Rubin, who is overseeing the publication of this revised edition; they're both great publishers and friends.

As always, special thanks to my most frequent companions, John H. Willoughby, John Ringwald, and Alisa Smith, and my agent Angela Miller—all of them give me invaluable love and perspective. Many other friends have been there for me in recent years: David Paskin, Pamela Hort, Semeon Tsalbins, Joe and Kim McGrath, Susan Moldow, Mitchell Orfuss, Naomi Glauberman, John Bancroft, Madeline Meacham, Fred Zolna, and Sherry Slade. My family has played a big role in inspiring and supporting me, and in eating the food I cook, like it or not. Though the days of raising a young family have passed for me, they are a constant reminder of the importance of cooking in daily life. I wish I could talk about this with the first great cook I knew, Helen Art, who would probably love The Minimalist—critically, of course.

Contents

Introduction

My philosophy has not changed much since I first wrote this introduction more than three years ago. I still believe that cooking simply brings not stress but enjoyment, as well as honesty, warmth, pleasure, modesty, even fairness. Simplicity in cooking is ease and grace.

Looking back on these first hundred or so recipes—all of which originated in my weekly *New York Times* column, "The Minimalist"—I'm happy about how contemporary they seem. But that's as it should be: Good, simple recipes are not trendy but timeless, or nearly so. What's different in this revised version of *The Minimalist Cooks at Home* is the addition of those elements that made its successor, *The Minimalist Cooks Dinner,* so popular: Serve with, wine pairings, more variations, and the tips I call "keys to success."

In general, these recipes require a minimum of technique and/or a minimum number of ingredients; most of them are fast as well. The approach is strictly less-is-more, an attempt to produce recipes that are so sophisticated, savvy, and fresh that they will inspire even experienced cooks while making them basic and simple enough to tempt novices.

The Minimalist Cooks at Home is more than a collection of columns, because I strongly believe that in every recipe there are the beginnings of many, many others. Almost every recipe offers opportunities for variations or spin-offs, techniques to be illustrated and explained in depth, lessons to be learned. I've taken advantage of the room offered in this book to expand each of the columns, to exploit the opportunities the recipes present.

A disproportionate amount of space and time in food magazines, newspapers, cookbooks, and television shows has been devoted to needlessly and sometimes outrageously complex recipes through a period where we are seeing the introduction of a new set of basic recipes, not the French classics revisited or the Italian staples revealed—although these are certainly parts of the trend—but the informal, quick, everyday food of households from all over the world.

In cultures where cooking is thousands of years old, most recipes are little more than combinations of the ingredients that appear seasonally. Now, for the first time in history, the standard ingredients of many of those cuisines are available in most supermarkets, opening new possibilities to both novice and experienced cooks. The result is that cooking no longer has to be complicated to be interesting and unusual. What's common to a home cook in Thailand is exotic to us; what's new is that the ingredients are sold in supermarkets, and the expertise needed to put them together is available in cookbooks like this one.

Thus, the recipes here not only provide great weeknight dinners. They (and those in the companion volume, *The Minimalist Cooks Dinner*) will change the repertoire of experienced cooks while demonstrating international cooking basics and teaching home cooks how to develop the sixth sense that comes with experience.

Again, it all starts with simplicity, which is not a compromise but a treasure.

Mark Bittman

Woodbridge, Connecticut

Fall 2001

The
MINIMALIST
Cooks at HOME

Soups

Lemongrass-Ginger Soup with Mushrooms

TIME: 30 minutes
MAKES: 4 servings

Nearly every American who was not raised in an Asian household flavors basic soup in pretty much the same way: with onions, carrots, celery, perhaps parsley or dill. There is nothing wrong with these essentially European flavors—in fact they have taken soup-making a long way—but Asian-flavored soups steer your palate in an entirely different direction. Here's a basic one, with plenty of possibilities.

6 cups good chicken stock

3 lemongrass stalks

4 nickel-sized slices fresh ginger

3 to 4 small hot chiles, minced, optional

2 tablespoons nam pla (fish sauce), or to taste

6 to 8 ounces roughly chopped oyster mushrooms

2 teaspoons minced lime leaves or lime zest

Juice of 1 lime

¼ cup minced cilantro leaves

1 Heat the stock over medium heat. Trim two of the lemongrass stalks of their toughest outer layers, then bruise them with the back of a knife; cut them into sections and add them to the stock with the ginger and about one-fourth of the minced chiles. Simmer for about 15 minutes, longer if you have the time. (You can prepare the recipe in advance up to this point; cover and refrigerate for up to 2 days before proceeding.)

2 Peel all of the hard layers off the remaining stalk of lemongrass and mince its tender inner core.

3 Remove the lemongrass and ginger. Add 1 tablespoon of the nam pla and the chopped mushrooms. Taste the broth and add more chiles if you like, as well as some salt if necessary. In the bottom of each of four warmed bowls, sprinkle a little chile, lime leaves or zest, lime juice, cilantro, and minced lemongrass.

4 Ladle the soup into the bowls and add a teaspoon of nam pla to each bowl. Serve piping hot.

WINE Gewürztraminer or other fruity, off-dry white, or Champagne; or beer.

SERVE WITH If you make some of the additions suggested in With Minimal Effort, the soup becomes practically an entire meal, especially if you serve it with some white rice. Otherwise, it's a good starter before any stir-fry, like that on page 122.

THIS THAI-FLAVORED SOUP, like most European soups, begins with chicken stock. You can use canned stock if you like, because the added ingredients here are so strong that all you really need from the base is a bit of body. (Good, homemade stock has better body than canned stock, of course; use it if you have it.)

YOU CAN FIND all of these ingredients in almost any supermarket, and if you don't have luck in yours, try an Asian market, where they are as common as carrots, celery, and onions. You don't need oyster mushrooms, by the way—fresh shiitakes or even white button mushrooms are just as good. All you really need to know is that lemongrass must be trimmed of its outer layers before mincing and nam pla (fish sauce) keeps forever in your pantry (and tastes much better than it smells).

YOU CAN MAKE this well in advance if you like, adding the final seasonings when you're ready to eat.

Lemongrass-Ginger Soup with Chicken: Add about 2 cups of cubed skinless, boneless chicken during the last 10 minutes of cooking (it's easier to remove the ginger and lemongrass stalks before adding the meat).

Lemongrass-Ginger Soup with Shrimp: Peel about 1 pound shrimp; devein if you like, and cut into bite-sized chunks (small shrimp may be left whole). Add to the stock during the last 5 minutes of cooking (it's easier to remove the ginger and lemongrass stalks before adding the shrimp).

■ Add cooked noodles, especially rice or bean-thread noodles, just long enough to heat through.

■ Add cooked vegetables, cut into small bits—asparagus, broccoli, watercress, and cabbage are especially good—just before serving.

■ Add raw vegetables, like bean sprouts or snow peas, just a minute or two before the end of cooking.

■ Add cubed soft or firm tofu a minute or two before the end of cooking.

Egg Drop Soup and Stracciatella

Egg Drop Soup

Egg drop soup, a cliché in American-Chinese restaurants for at least fifty years, has a less well-known Italian counterpart, called stracciatella. Both are based on the simple fact that eggs scramble or curdle in boiling water or stock, and each demonstrates the ease with which a basic dish can be transformed in spirit, moving from one cuisine to the other almost as quickly as you can change your mind about which you prefer.

4 cups chicken stock

4 eggs

1 tablespoon soy sauce, or to taste

Salt and freshly ground black pepper

½ cup chopped scallions, both white and green parts

1 teaspoon sesame oil, or to taste

1 Bring 3 cups of the stock to a boil over medium-high heat in a 6- to 8-cup saucepan. Beat the remaining stock with the eggs, cheese, nutmeg, and parsley until well blended.

2 When the stock is boiling, adjust the heat so that it bubbles frequently but not furiously. Add the egg mixture in a steady stream, stirring all the while. Stir occasionally until the eggs gather together in small curds, 2 or 3 minutes.

3 Add salt and pepper to taste, then serve. Garnish with a little more Parmesan if you like.

WINE Like many Chinese dishes, Egg Drop Soup is best with beer. Stracciatella is a different story, however, and is wonderful with a hearty red like Barolo (or anything else made with the nebbiolo grape) or Cabernet.

SERVE WITH These are clearly starters, and can be followed by any dish in the same spirit—stir-fries in the case of Egg Drop Soup, pasta or a simply cooked meat, chicken, or fish—try Chicken under a Brick, for example, page 102—and salad after Stracciatella.

TIME: 15 minutes
MAKES: 4 servings

Stracciatella

4 cups chicken stock

4 eggs

4 tablespoons freshly grated
Parmesan cheese

A tiny grating of fresh nutmeg

2 tablespoons minced parsley

Salt and freshly ground black
pepper

1 Bring 3 cups of the stock to a boil over medium-high heat in a 6- to 8-cup saucepan. Beat the remaining stock with the eggs, cheese, nutmeg, and parsley until well blended.

2 When the stock is boiling, adjust the heat so that it bubbles frequently but not furiously. Add the egg mixture in a steady stream, stirring all the while. Stir occasionally until the eggs gather together in small curds, 2 or 3 minutes.

3 Taste and add salt and pepper to taste, then serve. Garnish with a little more Parmesan if you like.

Keys To SUCCESS

WHEN YOU USE EGGS to thicken a sauce or stew, you keep the heat low in order to gain a smooth, creamy result. In egg drop soup, whether Chinese or Italian, you do just the opposite—keep the heat relatively high so the eggs cook in shreds, or curds. The result is a lightning-fast soup of substance.

EGG DROP SOUP is best flavored with soy sauce, plenty of chopped scallions, and a bit of sesame oil. Stracciatella is flavored with freshly grated Parmesan cheese (the real thing, Parmigiano-Reggiano, is essential here for best flavor) and a suspicion of garlic; some chopped parsley is an untraditional but pleasant addition.

BOTH THESE SOUPS rely on stock—you cannot make them of water and expect them to taste like anything—but the results are pretty good even with canned stock.

With MINIMAL Effort

Stracciatella with Greens: Add 2 cups chopped collards, kale, spinach, or watercress, to the simmering stock before stirring in the eggs. Spinach will cook almost instantly; the others will take a few minutes to become tender. Proceed as above.

Both of these soups are quite filling, but to make either into a one-pot meal:

■ Add about 2 cups finely chopped boneless chicken or peeled shrimp to either soup just before the eggs; they may be raw or cooked—either way. Cook just a minute or two.

■ Add about 2 cups cooked thin egg noodles or rice to either soup. (If you use rice, add a couple tablespoons of lemon juice; you'll have Greek-dinner egg-lemon soup.)

Garlic Soup with Shrimp

TIME: 30 minutes
MAKES: 4 servings

Most soups have simple origins, but none more so than this one of southern France, whose name translates as boiled water. At its most impoverished, this is no more than garlic simmered in water to give it flavor, with a few crusts of bread added for bulk. Simple as it is, boiled water is the perfect example of how an almost absurdly elementary preparation can be quickly and easily converted into one that is nearly grand.

¼ cup extra virgin olive oil

8 to 16 medium-to-large garlic cloves, peeled

Salt and freshly ground black pepper

4 thick slices French or Italian bread

6 cups shrimp stock (see page 7), chicken stock, water, or a combination

1 to 1½ pounds shrimp, peeled

Minced parsley leaves for garnish, optional

1 Combine the olive oil and garlic in a deep skillet or broad saucepan, turn the heat to medium, and sprinkle lightly with salt and pepper to taste. Cook, turning the garlic cloves occasionally until they are tender and lightly browned all over, about 10 minutes; lower the heat if they seem to be browning too quickly. Remove the garlic with a slotted spoon.

2 Turn the heat to low and add the bread (in batches if necessary); cook on each side until nicely browned, a total of about 4 minutes. Remove the bread, add the stock, and raise the heat to medium-high.

3 When the stock is nearly boiling, add the shrimp and salt and pepper to taste. Cook until the shrimp are pink, about 4 minutes. Place a piece of bread and a portion of garlic in each of 4 bowls, then ladle in a portion of soup and shrimp. Sprinkle with the optional parsley and serve.

WINE Chianti, Zinfandel, or a rough red from the south of France.

SERVE WITH Serve with a salad for a nice light dinner.

COOK THE GARLIC very gently in order to add complexity and color; by then browning the bread in the same oil, you increase its flavor immeasurably. Also consider doubling the amount of bread given in the recipe here; like me, you may find the allure of bread crisped in garlic-scented oil irresistible.

USE STOCK in place of water if you have it. This is a great place for canned stock, because the garlic-scented oil will boost it to a higher level. Or you can make a stock from the shrimp shells: Put the shells in a pot, cover with water, bring to a boil, and simmer for about five minutes; strain. (The liquid can be used in many shrimp dishes, or in place of fish stock in most recipes. You can accumulate shells and freeze them over a period of months if you like, and there's no need to defrost them before making the stock.) The amount of stock made by the pound or so of shrimp in this recipe isn't enough to complete the soup, but its volume can be increased with water or enhanced with chicken stock; the combination is wonderful.

Spicy Garlic Soup: To make the soup even more flavorful, brown a little spice in the oil after removing the bread and before adding the stock. I especially like a combination of cumin and paprika (about a teaspoon of each), which gives the soup a decidedly Spanish feeling. Curry powder, mild chili powder, a pinch of cayenne, or a few rosemary leaves are all possibilities, too; this is a good place to experiment.

Thai Garlic Soup: Add a minced fresh chile, or a few dried chiles, to the oil along with the garlic (discard dried chiles after cooking). Omit the bread; add 2 cups cooked rice to the soup along with the shrimp. Substitute cilantro for the parsley, and serve with wedges of lime.

Meaty Garlic Soup: Substitute 2 cups boneless chicken or pork, cut into ½-inch chunks, for the shrimp; cooking time will be about the same.

Carrot-Garlic Soup: Substitute 2 cups peeled carrots, cut into ½-inch chunks, for the shrimp; cooking time will be about 10 minutes.

Prosciutto Soup

Water-based soups are great, but soups with character are best when made with meat stocks. Of course you don't always have stock, and there are shortcuts that produce in-between soups. One of the easiest and most effective ways of making a potent soup quickly and without stock is to start with a small piece of prosciutto or other dry-cured ham, like Smithfield. The long aging process this meat undergoes—almost always a year or more—ensures an intense flavor that is quickly transferred to anything in which it is cooked, including water.

3 tablespoons extra virgin olive oil

¼ pound prosciutto, in 1 chunk or slice

4 garlic cloves

1 medium onion

½ pound greens, such as spinach or kale

¾ cup small pasta, such as orzo or small shells

Salt and freshly ground black pepper

1 Set 6 cups water to boil. Put 2 tablespoons of the olive oil in the bottom of a medium saucepan and turn the heat to medium. Chop the prosciutto (remove the fat if you must, but remember that it has flavor) into ¼-inch or smaller cubes, and add to the oil. Brown, stirring occasionally, for about 5 minutes, while you prepare the garlic, onion, and greens.

2 Peel the garlic and chop it roughly or leave it whole. Peel and chop the onion. Wash and chop the greens into bite-sized pieces.

3 When the prosciutto has browned, add the garlic and cook, stirring occasionally, until it begins to color, about 2 minutes. Add the onion and cook, stirring occasionally, until it becomes translucent, 2 or 3 minutes. Add the greens and stir, then add the 6 cups boiling water. (You can prepare the dish in advance up to this point. Cover and refrigerate for up to 2 days, then reheat before proceeding.) Stir in the pasta and a good sprinkling of salt and pepper; adjust the heat so the mixture simmers.

WINE Rough and red, like Chianti.

SERVE WITH As you can see from the above, it's easy enough to make this into something approaching a whole-meal soup, in which case all you need is some bread. Otherwise it makes a great starter before pasta like Ziti with Butter, Sage, and Parmesan, page 44.

4 When the pasta is done, taste and add more salt and pepper if necessary. Drizzle with the remaining olive oil and serve.

Keys To SUCCESS

TO SAVE TIME, chop the vegetables and add them one at a time while you're rendering the ham; by the time you're done chopping, you'll have added all the ingredients except water. And if you bring the water to a boil before you begin chopping, you really minimize cooking time, producing a thick, rich soup in less than thirty minutes.

THE BASIC RECIPE HERE, though delicious, is on the meager side, the kind of soup people make either when times are hard or no one's been shopping lately: a small piece of meat, some common vegetables, a little pasta. But you can make it as elaborate as you like, and even convert it to a stew by doubling the amount of meat, vegetables, and pasta; the chopping time will be extended slightly, but the cooking time will remain more or less the same.

DO NOT OMIT the final drizzle of olive oil; its freshness really brings this soup to life. In fact, if you have a bottle of oil that you reserve for special uses, consider this one of them and break it out.

With MINIMAL Effort

This soup is fair game for whatever you have around, and almost every ingredient can be swapped for something else. The only essential components are the prosciutto, olive oil, and, of course, water.

■ Add more root vegetables, like thin-sliced carrots or chopped celery, or small-cut potatoes or turnips.

■ Vary the greens: Shredded cabbage is perfect for this soup, and will cook as quickly as kale. Collard, mustard, or turnip greens are also appropriate. Some peas and/or corn work nicely, too, even if they come from the freezer.

■ Use any starch you like in place of the pasta: Rice and barley, each of which may take a few minutes longer than pasta, are the best choices.

■ Add tomatoes, either fresh, canned, or paste, for color and flavor. To use tomato paste, just stir a couple of tablespoons into the sautéing vegetables before adding the water. Tomatoes should be added with the onions, so they have time to break up.

■ Leftovers are great, like a bit of chopped chicken, or some vegetables from a previous meal (rinse them with boiling water if they were sauced).

■ Consider the chopped-up rind of hard cheese, such as Parmesan, which will not only soften enough to become edible during cooking but will add great flavor to the soup.

Turkey Stock

TIME: About 2½ hours, largely unattended

MAKES: About 2 quarts

Most turkey meat finds its way into sandwiches, but many cooks make a turkey soup as well, tossing the bones with some of the leftover meat into a pot with water to cover and simmering until the meat falls off the bones—a technique that produces quite decent results.

However, there's a nearly-as-simple method that allows you to produce dark, rich turkey stock in the turkey roasting pan. This broth has a broader range of uses than the throw-everything-in-the-pot variety; in fact, the result is very close to jus roti, the dark stock of classic French cooking.

Bones, leftover meat, and carcass from a 15-pound turkey

2 carrots, peeled and cut into chunks

1 large onion, peeled and quartered

1 celery stalk, roughly chopped

1 Preheat the over to 450°F. Place the bones, meat, and chopped carcass in a large roasting pan and put in the oven. Roast, stirring occasionally, for about 1 hour, or until nicely browned. Don't worry if the meat sticks to the bottom of the pan.

2 Add the chopped vegetables and roast for about 30 minutes more, stirring once or twice.

3 Move the roasting pan to the stovetop and place it over one or two burners, whichever is more convenient. Turn the heat to high and add water to barely cover the bones, about 8 to 10 cups; don't worry if some of the bones poke up out of the water. When the water boils, turn the heat down so that the liquid simmers.

4 Cook, stirring occasionally and scraping the bottom of the pan to loosen any bits of meat, for about 30 minutes. Cool, then strain. Refrigerate and skim off excess fat, then store for up to 3 days in the refrigerator (longer if you bring the stock to a boil every second day) or several months in the freezer.

WINE The broth itself can be served with a good white or red Burgundy, or even a slightly sweet wine. If you add to it, choose a wine suited to the character of the additions.

SERVE WITH See With Minimal Effort; as a stock, it can go in many directions.

TO MAKE BROWN STOCK, you brown (or, in culinary lingo, "caramelize") meat and vegetables, then simmer them with water. That's just what you do here: Take the leftover turkey, including bones, any meat you can spare, and the meaty carcass, and place them in the same roasting pan you used for the turkey; you need not even wash it first. Throw it in the oven and brown it; add vegetables, then water. With far more time than work you'll have a strong, sweet, and meaty turkey stock—good enough to eat unadulterated as clear broth, and a perfect base for almost any other soup.

YOU MUST CHOP or break the carcass into a few pieces before adding it to the pan or you will need too much water to cover it.

ALTHOUGH PRECISE MEASURING of vegetables is not essential, bear in mind that each has its own strong flavor, and an overabundance of one or all can throw the stock out of balance.

Roast Chicken Stock: Since a chicken carcass won't be as large, you'll have to either cut back on the water or add some fresh chicken; wings and/or legs are best. Otherwise proceed exactly as above.

There are dozens of additions you can make to the stock as it is cooking, or convert it into soup when it is done. Some quick ideas:

■ Throw a head of garlic, cut in half, into the roasting pan along with the other vegetables.

■ Add a small handful of mushrooms, or mushroom trimmings, or reconstituted dried mushrooms to the roasting pan along with the other vegetables.

■ Add stems and/or leaves of parsley or dill to the simmering stock; don't overdo it.

■ Add chopped vegetables, leftover turkey, and noodles or rice to the broth to turn it into a full-fledged soup.

■ To make tortellini in broth, gently simmer about 10 tortellini per serving in the stock until tender; garnish with freshly grated Parmesan cheese. You can do the same with ravioli.

■ To make mushroom-barley soup, add sliced fresh mushrooms, reconstituted dried mushrooms, and about ½ cup barley per 4 cups of stock; cook until the barley is tender.

■ To make minestrone, cook chopped tomatoes (canned are fine), cooked beans, minced vegetables, and small pasta in the stock until tender.

Pumpkin Soup

TIME: 40 minutes
MAKES: 4 servings

Usually, pumpkin means pie, a limited role for a large vegetable that is nearly ubiquitous from Labor Day through Christmas. But soup based on pumpkin—or other winter squash like acorn or butternut—is a minimalist's dream, a luxuriously creamy dish that requires little more than a stove and a blender.

Despite its simplicity, this soup is so good, it (or something very much like it) is served at swank restaurants all over the country; waiters proudly declare, "It's very creamy, but contains no cream at all." (I'll be the first to confess, however, that it is at least a little bit better with some cream—fresh or sour—added at the last minute.)

2 pounds peeled pumpkin or other winter squash (weighed after peeling; see page 13 for peeling instructions)

4 to 5 cups chicken or other stock

Salt and freshly ground black pepper

1 Place the pumpkin or squash in a saucepan with stock to cover and a pinch of salt. Turn the heat to high and bring to a boil. Cover and adjust the heat so that the mixture simmers. Cook until the pumpkin or squash is very tender, about 30 minutes. If time allows, cool.

2 Place the mixture, in batches if necessary, in the container of a blender and puree until smooth. (The recipe can be prepared a day or two in advance up to this point; cool, place in a covered container, and refrigerate.) Reheat, adjust seasoning, and serve.

WINE As long as it's white and dry, almost anything will do, from something light to a fine Burgundy.

SERVE WITH This is a very homey starter to a fall meal, and is perfect on Thanksgiving. See page 132 for The Minimalist's Thanksgiving Turkey.

IF THERE IS A CHALLENGE here, it lies in peeling the squash. The big mistake many people make is to attack it with a standard vegetable peeler; the usual result is an unpeeled pumpkin and a broken peeler. A quicker and more reliable method is to cut the squash up into wedges; then rest each section on a cutting board and use a sharp, heavy knife to cut away the peel. You'll wind up taking part of the flesh with it, but given the large size and small cost of winter squash, this is hardly a concern.

PUTTING THE SOUP TOGETHER is a snap: You combine peeled pumpkin or other winter squash with any good stock and simmer until the squash is soft—about thirty minutes. Then you puree in a blender and reheat, with or without seasonings or garnish. (If time allows, cool the mixture before pureeing, for safety's sake.)

Pumpkin and Apple Soup: This screams autumn: Add ½ teaspoon dried ginger or 1 teaspoon minced fresh ginger to the soup. Peel, core, and thinly slice 2 apples; cook them in 2 tablespoons butter until lightly browned, turning occasionally. Use the slices to garnish the soup.

Pumpkin and Mushroom Soup: Sauté about 1 cup sliced mushrooms—chanterelles are best, but shiitakes (discard the stems) or button mushrooms are good—in 2 tablespoons butter or extra virgin olive oil until they give up their liquid and begin to become crisp. Use to garnish the soup.

To make this basic soup more complex:

■ Add a teaspoon of ground ginger (or 1 tablespoon finely minced fresh ginger) or a teaspoon of curry powder (and, if you have it, ½ teaspoon of turmeric) to the simmering soup.

■ Add ½ teaspoon of cinnamon, ¼ teaspoon of allspice, and a small grating of nutmeg to the simmering soup.

■ Garnish each bowl of soup with three or four grilled, sautéed, or roasted shrimp; or about ¼ cup crabmeat or lobster meat per serving.

■ Garnish the soup with chopped chervil, chives, parsley, or dill.

■ Stir 2 tablespoons to 1 cup of crème fraîche, sweet cream, sour cream, or yogurt into the pureed soup as you are reheating it.

■ Stir about 1 cup of cooked long-grain rice into the pureed soup as you are reheating it.

Clam Chowder

Although clam chowder takes many guises, the best is a simple affair that has as its flavorful essence the juices of the clams themselves.

And as long as you begin with fresh clams, these juices are easily extracted and reserved; the minced clam meat becomes a garnish. Some onion and garlic are welcome, although only the former, I think, is essential. Diced potatoes are a near-necessary addition, for the body they lend. And I like finishing the chowder with a little cream—or at least milk—for both color and silkiness.

Of course, what is actually "essential" in clam chowder is debatable: Manhattanites, in theory at least, prefer theirs with tomatoes. New Englanders, we assume, like it with cream. There is also Rhode Island clam chowder, which in spirit at least is closest to the minimalist ideal: It contains clams, onion, celery, water, salt, and pepper.

At least 3 dozen littleneck clams (3 pounds or more), or an equivalent amount of other clams

1 medium onion, peeled and minced

2 large potatoes (about 1 pound), peeled and cut into ¼-inch dice

Salt and freshly ground black pepper

1 Wash the clams well, scrubbing if necessary to remove external grit. Place them in a pot with ½ cup water and turn the heat to high. Steam, shaking the pot occasionally, until most of the clams are open, 7 to 10 minutes. Use a slotted spoon to remove the clams to a broad bowl; reserve the cooking liquid.

2 When the clams are cool enough to handle, shuck them over the bowl, catching every drop of their liquid; discard the shells. If any clams remain closed, use a thin-bladed knife to pry them open (it will be easy).

3 Chop the clams. Strain all the liquid through a sieve lined with a paper towel or a couple of layers of cheesecloth. Measure the liquid and add enough water to make 3½ cups. (You may prepare the dish in advance up to this point; refrigerate, covered, for up to a day before reheating.)

Combine the liquid with the onion and potatoes in a saucepan; cover and bring to a boil. Reduce to a simmer, still covered, and cook until the potatoes are tender, about 10 minutes. Stir in the clams, season to taste with salt and pepper, and serve.

WINE Chardonnay, not necessarily an expensive one, is best.

SERVE WITH A great starter for any seafood meal, especially Spice-Rubbed Salmon, page 81.

BEGIN WITH THE RIGHT CLAMS. Any hard-shell clam—larger ones are called cherrystones or quahogs, smaller ones littlenecks—will do, because they're easy to clean and contain little if any sand in their interior. (Although the meat of the larger clams is tough, this is not a huge issue here because it will be diced.) The cockles seen in some fish markets these days, which resemble small clams, are also good. Steamers contain so much sand that some will inevitably find its way into your broth.

WHEN BUYING HARD-SHELL CLAMS, remember that live ones have tightly closed shells; reject any whose shells are open or cracked. Those that do not open fully during steaming are perfectly fine; simply pry them open with a knife.

New England Clam Chowder: Add ½ cup or more of milk, cream, or half-and-half along with the chopped clams.

Manhattan Clam Chowder: Add 1 cup peeled, seeded, and diced tomatoes (canned are fine) to the steaming water.

Rhode Island Clam Chowder: Replace the potatoes with ½ cup minced celery.

■ Substitute white wine for the water in the initial steaming.

■ Add 3 crushed garlic cloves to the steaming water; discard them with the clam shells.

■ Garnish the chowder with minced parsley or other herbs.

Cold Tomato Soup with Rosemary

TIME: 15 minutes, plus time to chill

MAKES: 4 servings

Good tomatoes are bursting with potential. The difference between consuming a tomato out of hand and slicing it, then sprinkling it with a pinch of salt and a few drops of olive oil, is the difference between a snack and a dish. And the great thing about tomatoes is that it takes so little to convert them from one to the other.

This soup is a great example, an almost instant starter that requires no cooking at all. It benefits from a period of chilling after being put together, but if you use ice cubes in place of chicken stock (or combine the two) you can even skip that.

2 slices good stale white bread, crusts removed

3 pounds ripe tomatoes, peeled, seeded, and roughly chopped

1 teaspoon fresh rosemary leaves

1 small garlic clove, peeled

1 cup chicken stock or ice cubes

Salt and freshly ground black pepper

Juice of 1 lemon or more to taste

1 Soak the bread in cold water briefly; squeeze dry and combine in a blender with the tomatoes, rosemary, and garlic (you may have to do this in two batches). Add the ice cubes if using them. Turn on the machine and drizzle in the stock. Turn off the machine and pour the mixture into a bowl.

2 Season with salt and pepper to taste, then add lemon juice. Chill and serve.

WINE Beaujolais, lightly chilled, or another light red.

SERVE WITH The perfect starter for a summer meal of almost anything; try, for example, Grilled Tuna with Mesclun Stuffing, page 78, or Perfect Grilled Steak, page 140.

TOMATOES SHOULD ALWAYS be cored before using. With a paring knife, cut a cone-shaped wedge out of the stem end and remove it.

IN THIS INSTANCE—though not always—peeling and seeding the tomatoes are worth the effort as well. To do so, bring a pot of water to a boil. Meanwhile, cut a small X on the smooth (flower) end of each tomato. Drop them into the boiling water. In about thirty seconds, you'll see the skin begin to loosen. Immediately remove from the boiling water and plunge into a bowl of ice water. When they're cool, peel, then cut them in half through their equator. Squeeze and shake out the seeds. (For best flavor, do this over a strainer and recombine the reserved juices with the pulp.)

■ Use fresh thyme (1 teaspoon), dill (1 tablespoon), basil (¼ cup), parsley (¼ cup), chervil (1 tablespoon), chives (¼ cup), or a mixture of herbs. Garnish with fresh herbs, too, if you like.

■ Finish the dish with a sprinkling of top-quality extra virgin olive oil.

■ Substitute a shallot or a small handful of chives for the garlic.

Tomato-Melon Gazpacho

TIME: 20 minutes, plus time to chill

MAKES: 4 servings

I like gazpacho, but the ultimate minimalist version—take a few tomatoes, a red pepper, some onion, oil, and vinegar, and whiz it in a blender—doesn't cut it for me. I find this pulverized salad coarse, its raw flavor strong and altogether too lingering.

I have tried many variations, many of them traditional—roasting the vegetables first to reduce their rawness, using almonds, cucumbers, even grapes to lighten the flavor, letting the mixture sit to meld the flavors. None really did the trick.

Then the great chef, my friend and sometimes co-author Jean-Georges Vongerichten, suggested that I abandon tradition entirely and combine tomatoes with another fruit of the season: cantaloupe. These, combined with basil and lemon—in place of vinegar—produce the mildest, most delicious, creamiest gazpacho I've ever tasted. With its bright orange color, it's also among the most beautiful.

4 tomatoes, about 1½ pounds
One 3-pound cantaloupe
2 tablespoons olive oil
1½ cups of water or 1 cup water and ½ cup ice cubes
10 basil leaves
Salt and freshly ground black pepper
Juice of a lemon

1 Core, peel, and seed the tomatoes; cut the flesh into 1-inch chunks. Seed the melon and remove the flesh from the rind; cut into chunks. Place a tablespoon of olive oil in each of two 10- or 12-inch skillets and turn the heat under both to high (you can do this sequentially if you have only one skillet). Add the melon to one skillet and the tomatoes to the other and cook, stirring, until they become juicy, no longer than 2 minutes.

2 In a blender, puree the melon, tomato, water, and basil, along with some salt, pepper, and the remaining olive oil. Chill, then add lemon juice to taste and adjust seasoning. Serve.

WINE A full-bodied white, preferably a decent Burgundy.
SERVE WITH Definitely a starter, great before grilled meat (or Grilled Lobster, page 86) and a salad.

Keys To SUCCESS

FOR THE BEST POSSIBLE SOUP, both tomato and melon must be perfectly ripe.

COOL THE MIXTURE at least slightly after cooking, and puree until creamy.

With MINIMAL Effort

- Substitute about ½ cup mint for the basil.

- Garnish with melon balls, or those scooped from a seeded cucumber.

Creamy Broccoli Soup and Potato and Onion Soup

It isn't often that you can apply a simple formula to a broad range of dishes, but when it comes to creamy vegetable soups—whether hot or cold—there is one that actually works. The soups have three basic ingredients, and their proportions form a pyramid: three parts liquid, two parts vegetable, one part dairy.

The pyramid's foundation is chicken stock (you can substitute vegetable stock or water, but the result will be somewhat less substantial). The middle section is any vegetable, or combination of vegetables, that will puree nicely and produce good body and flavor. The peak is cream, or nearly any other dairy product—milk, yogurt, or sour cream.

To make four servings, the three-two-one measurement is in cups, conveniently enough, because a total of six cups is the perfect amount of soup for four people.

Creamy Broccoli Soup

2 cups broccoli florets and peeled stems (about ½ average head), cut into chunks

3 cups chicken stock

1 garlic clove, peeled and cut in half

1 cup milk, cream, or yogurt

Salt and freshly ground black pepper

1 Combine the broccoli and the stock in a saucepan and simmer, covered, until the broccoli is tender, about 10 minutes. During the last minute or so of cooking, add the garlic (this cooks the garlic just enough to remove its raw taste). If you're serving the soup cold, chill now (or refrigerate for up to 2 days, or freeze for up to a month before proceeding).

2 Puree in a blender, in batches if necessary, until very smooth. Stir in the milk, cream, or yogurt and reheat gently (or chill again); do not boil. Season to taste and serve.

WINE Almost always white, usually crisp and unpretentious; something inexpensive and clean.

SERVE WITH In summer, serve chilled with bread and salad for a light meal. In cold weather, these are hearty starters.

ALWAYS COOK the vegetables until very tender, but no more than that. Spinach is tender in a couple of minutes; potatoes, cut into chunks, will require ten or fifteen. Almost nothing will take longer than that. Cover the pot while the vegetables cook to prevent too much of the stock from evaporating.

SEASONINGS THAT REQUIRE COOKING, like garlic and onions, should be added with the vegetables. Those that do not, like herbs and spices, are best added before pureeing the cold mixture so they retain their freshness. Generally speaking, cold soups require more seasoning than hot ones.

LEFTOVER VEGETABLES are super candidates for this soup. Rinse off any remnants of dressing with hot water, then combine with stock and puree.

WHEN YOU PUREE in a blender, do so in batches if necessary, and make sure the blender lid is on securely to avoid scalding.

ALWAYS REHEAT GENTLY, especially if you're using yogurt, which will curdle if it boils; or chill to serve cold.

SOME VEGETABLES—like winter squash—are so dense that they create their own creaminess, reducing the amount of dairy needed in the final step. (See page 12.)

The possible combinations for creamy vegetable soups are literally infinite; here are ten suggestions you can use following the general guidelines and recipes above:

- **Beet.** Add some minced scallion or chive. Puree with sour cream and garnish with chives and a teaspoon of sour cream per serving.

- **Spinach.** Start with 10 to 16 ounces leaves (remove thick stems). Cook quickly, adding a bit of garlic if you like.

- **Turnip and parsnip.** Or turnip and potato. Cook with a small onion and some thyme.

- **Red pepper and tomato.** Peel and seed both before cooking. Puree with sour cream to thicken the mixture, which will be thin. Garnish with chervil (ideally) or parsley.

- **Carrot.** Nice with a pinch of cayenne and a teaspoon or more of minced ginger.

- **Cucumber.** Don't cook, but peel the cucumbers, cut them in half, and scoop out seeds before combining with stock. Use sour cream and plenty of fresh dill.

- **Peas or snow peas.** Make sure to remove the strings from snow peas. Cook with thyme or mint.

- **Celery or fennel.** Cook a few cloves of garlic along with the vegetable.

- **Artichoke hearts.** If you use canned hearts, simply puree with cold chicken stock; there's no need to cook.

- **Tomatillos or green tomatoes.** Season with chili powder, puree with sour cream, and garnish with a teaspoon of sour cream.

Potato and Onion Soup

1 cup potato (about 1 large), peeled and cut into chunks

1 cup onion or leeks, peeled or trimmed, washed if necessary, and cut into chunks

3 cups chicken stock

1 cup milk or cream

Salt and freshly ground black pepper

Chopped parsley leaves or chives for garnish

1 Combine the potato, onion or leeks, and stock in a saucepan and simmer, covered, until the potato is tender, about 15 minutes. If you're serving the soup cold, chill now (or refrigerate for up to 2 days, or freeze for up to a month before proceeding).

2 Puree in a blender, in batches if necessary, until very smooth. Stir in the milk or cream and reheat gently (or chill again); do not boil. Season to taste, garnish with the parsley or chives, and serve.

GRILLED BREAD SALAD

PEAR AND GORGONZOLA GREEN SALAD

ASIAN CHICKEN SALAD

CUCUMBER SALAD WITH SCALLOPS

MINTY BROILED SHRIMP SALAD

Salads

Grilled Bread Salad

Bread salad is a way of making good use of stale bread. The bread is softened, usually with water, olive oil, lemon juice, or a combination, then tossed with tomatoes and a variety of seasonings. Like many old-fashioned preparations created as a way to salvage food before it goes bad (count pickles and jam among these), bread salad has an appeal of its own. This is especially true in the summer, when good tomatoes are plentiful.

1 small baguette (about 8 ounces) or other crusty bread

¼ cup extra virgin olive oil

¼ cup fresh lemon juice (good vinegar also works well)

2 tablespoons diced shallot, scallion, or red onion

¼ teaspoon minced garlic, optional

1½ pounds tomatoes, chopped

Salt and freshly ground black pepper

¼ cup or more roughly chopped basil or parsley

1 Start a gas or charcoal grill or preheat the broiler; the rack should be 4 to 6 inches from the heat source. Cut the bread lengthwise into quarters. Grill or broil the bread, watching carefully and turning as each side browns and chars slightly; total time will be less than 10 minutes.

2 While the bread cools, mix together the next five ingredients in a large bowl. Mash the tomatoes with the back of a fork to release all of their juices. Season to taste with salt and pepper. Cut the bread into ½- to 1-inch cubes (no larger) and toss it with the dressing.

3 Let the bread sit for 20 to 30 minutes, tossing occasionally and tasting a piece every now and then. The salad is at its peak when the bread is fairly soft but some edges remain crisp, but you can serve it before or after it reaches that state. When it's ready, stir in the herb and serve.

WINE Red and spicy, like Zinfandel or any of the southern Rhône varietals.

SERVE WITH Because it's juicy, almost saucy, and pleasantly acidic, this salad makes a nice accompaniment to simple grilled meat or poultry, and has a special affinity for dark fish such as tuna and swordfish.

YOU CAN WAIT AROUND for bread to go stale, but the best way to ready bread for salad is to use the grill or broiler to dry the bread quickly while charring the edges slightly, adding another dimension of flavor to the salad. But watch the bread carefully as you grill or broil it; a slight char is good, but it's a short step from there to burned bread.

THE TIME YOU ALLOW the bread to soften after tossing it with the seasonings varies some; keep tasting until the texture pleases you. If your tomatoes are on the dry side, you might add a little extra liquid, in the form of more olive oil and lemon juice, or a light sprinkling of water.

Bread Salad with Shrimp, Chicken, or Tuna:
For a one-dish meal, grill or broil some shrimp or boneless chicken alongside the bread, then add the chunks to the salad. Or add some leftover or canned tuna (the Italian kind, packed in olive oil) to the mix.

This is a substantial salad, but it's still a side dish unless you're in the mood for a very light meal. But there are some options:

■ Before grilling, rub the bread with a cut clove of garlic and/or brush it with some olive oil and a sprinkle of salt.

■ Add to the salad ¼ cup chopped olives, 1 tablespoon capers, and/or 2 minced anchovy fillets.

Pear and Gorgonzola Green Salad

As far a cry from iceberg lettuce and bottled dressing as you can imagine, but not much more work, this is a magical combination of powerful flavors made without cooking or any major challenges. No wonder it's become a classic.

2 large pears, about 1 pound
1 tablespoon lemon juice
4 ounces Gorgonzola or other creamy blue cheese

6 cups mixed greens, washed, dried, and torn into bite-sized pieces
About ½ cup Basic Vinaigrette, page 186, made with balsamic vinegar

1 Peel and core the pears; cut them into ½-inch chunks and toss with the lemon juice. Cover and refrigerate until needed, up to 2 hours.
2 Crumble the Gorgonzola into small bits; cover and refrigerate until needed.
3 When you're ready to serve, toss the pears, cheese, and greens together with as much of the dressing as you like. Serve immediately.

WINE Vinegar makes for difficult wine pairings, but if you're not too put off by this, try a not-too-austere Cabernet Sauvignon or Merlot.

SERVE WITH This rich salad can serve as the centerpiece of a light lunch, accompanied by little more than bread. It makes an equally great starter for a grand dinner—followed by roasted meat or fish, for example—or a simple meal, served with a soup.

SIMPLE AS THIS SALAD IS, without top-quality ingredients it won't amount to much. So:

USE SHERRY or good balsamic vinegar to make Basic Vinaigrette (page 186).

THE PEARS must be tender and very juicy, so sample one before making the salad—it should not be crunchy, mushy, or dry.

THE GORGONZOLA should be creamy; ask for a taste before buying it.

Pear and Gorgonzola Salad with Walnuts: To add another dimension—crunchiness—place 1 cup walnuts in a dry skillet with the heat on medium, and toast them, shaking the pan frequently, until they are aromatic and beginning to darken in color, 3 to 5 minutes. Set aside to cool while you prepare the other ingredients, then crumble them into bits over the salad. Try hazelnuts, too.

■ Substitute spinach, arugula, or any other strong-flavored salad green for the mesclun.

■ Add about a cup of diced cucumber or bell pepper (preferably red or yellow) to the greens when you toss them.

■ Crumble about ½ cup of crisp-cooked bacon over the salad in place of or along with the walnuts.

■ Omit the pears; just make a salad of greens and cheese. Nuts are great here, too.

Asian Chicken Salad

TIME: 30 to 40 minutes (longer if you
want to serve the salad cold)
MAKES: 4 servings

The standard chicken salad—poached chicken, mayonnaise, and celery—is about as minimalist as you can get, but I prefer one that has only one thing—chicken—in common with the familiar variety. This one features grilled chicken; a super-flavorful dressing based on soy sauce, peanut or sesame butter, and spices; and cucumber for crunch. Make extra dressing and you can serve the chicken on top of a bed of salad greens.

1½ pounds boneless, skinless chicken thighs or breasts

3 tablespoons soy sauce

1½ tablespoons peanut butter or tahini (ground sesame paste)

1 teaspoon roasted sesame oil

1 small garlic clove, peeled

A few drops of hot sauce, such as Tabasco

Salt and freshly ground black pepper

¼ teaspoon sugar

1 tablespoon rice or other mild vinegar

1 cucumber

½ cup minced cilantro leaves

1 Start a charcoal or gas grill, or preheat the broiler. Cut the chicken meat into ½- to 1-inch chunks and thread it onto skewers (if you're broiling you can forget the skewers and simply use a roasting pan). Put the skewers on a plate and drizzle with 2 tablespoons of the soy sauce.

2 In a blender, combine the remaining soy sauce with the peanut butter, sesame oil, garlic, hot sauce, salt and pepper to taste, sugar, and vinegar. Turn the blender on and add hot water, a teaspoon at a time, until the mixture is smooth and creamy. (You will not need more than 3 teaspoons of water.)

3 Grill or broil the chicken, turning once or twice. Total cooking time will be 6 to 8 minutes for breasts, 10 to 12

WINE Something with fizz, like Champagne or beer, or a not-too-dry Riesling or Gewürztraminer.

SERVE WITH Rice salad, with a lightly vinegared dressing and some finely chopped vegetables, would be ideal, though this salad served with greens (see With Minimal Effort) makes a good whole meal in itself.

minutes for thighs. Meanwhile, peel the cucumber (if it is waxed), slice it in half the long way, and scoop out the seeds with a spoon. Cut it into ½-inch dice and combine in a bowl with the sauce. When the chicken is done, toss it with the sauce and cucumber. Taste and adjust seasoning if necessary, then serve hot or cold, garnished with the cilantro.

Asian Chicken Salad with Greens: To make this into a larger salad, wash and dry 6 cups salad greens. Double the quantities for the dressing. After blending, remove half of the mixture and combine with the cucumber and chicken as above; chill. To the remaining dressing in the blender, add about ⅓ cup hot water, and blend until well combined. Toss the dressing with the greens, top with the chicken and cucumber, garnish, and serve.

- Add minced bell pepper (preferably red or yellow), celery, and/or zucchini to the mix.

- Garnish with basil (Thai basil is especially good), mint, or minced scallions in place of or in addition to the cilantro.

Keys To SUCCESS

BY COMBINING THE CHICKEN and sauce while the chicken is hot, the flavors marry perfectly, and their clarity remains even after the chicken has been chilled. (Of course you can serve the dish hot or warm if you prefer.)

BONELESS CHICKEN THIGHS are preferable to breasts, because their flavor and texture are superior, they remain moist during grilling, and they brown perfectly.

I LIMIT THE HOT SAUCE to a few drops, but obviously you can add as much as you like; garlic, vinegar, and sesame oil also can be added to taste. Unless you must omit it for health reasons, you should really include the sugar, which even in this minuscule quantity adds a certain roundness that is otherwise lacking.

Cucumber Salad
with Scallops

TIME: About 1 hour (somewhat unattended)

MAKES: 4 servings

Sometimes a simple salad features such powerful flavors that by adding a couple of straightforward ingredients, a whole meal appears as if by magic. Here, the starting place is a Southeast Asian–style cucumber salad, with a dressing made from lime juice, lemongrass, fish sauce (called nam pla in Thailand and nuoc mam in Vietnam), and a few other strong seasonings. This dressing commingles perfectly with the natural juices of the cucumbers to moisten the greens. Top all with grilled scallops—or other fish or meat—and you create an easy one-dish meal whose flavor really jumps off the plate. It looks lovely, too, especially if your cucumbers are good enough to leave unpeeled. And (although not by design, I assure you), this salad is extremely low in fat.

4 medium cucumbers, at least 2 pounds

Salt

2 tablespoons nam pla (fish sauce)

Juice of 2 limes

1 small garlic clove, very finely minced

Crushed red pepper flakes or finely minced fresh chiles

1 tablespoon minced lemongrass

½ teaspoon sugar

6 cups mixed salad greens

1 to 1½ pounds sea scallops

1 tablespoon neutral oil, such as canola or grapeseed

⅛ teaspoon cayenne pepper

½ cup chopped mint, cilantro, basil, or a combination

2 teaspoons dark sesame oil

1 Peel the cucumbers if they have been waxed, then trim their ends and cut them in half the long way. Scoop out the seeds with an ordinary teaspoon. Sprinkle each half with about ¼ teaspoon salt, then place them all in a colander. Let drain for about 30 minutes. Rinse lightly and drain again. Cut into ⅛- to ¼-inch-thick slices and place in a bowl.

2 Mix together the fish sauce, lime juice, garlic, red pepper flakes to taste, lemongrass, and sugar. Thin with a tablespoon of water. Taste and add more of any flavoring you wish. Toss the dressing with the cucumbers and set aside while you proceed with the recipe.

3 Place the greens on a large platter. Put a large nonstick skillet over high heat. Toss the scallops with the oil, then sprinkle them with salt and the cayenne. When the skillet begins to smoke, add the scallops, one at a time and

WINE This is so highly seasoned that it will overwhelm any wine; go with beer.

SERVE WITH You need nothing, but if you want something starchy, some cold noodles tossed with the sauce for Asian Chicken Salad (page 28) would be great.

without crowding, until they are all in the pan. Cook for about 2 minutes on the first side, turning as they brown; depending on their size, cook for 1 to 3 minutes on the second side. (Scallops are best when their interior is slightly underdone; cut into one to check it.)

4 Toss the cucumbers with most of the herbs and spoon them and all of their juices over the greens. Top with the scallops. Drizzle with the sesame oil and top with the remaining herbs. Serve immediately.

Keys To SUCCESS

IF SOME OF THESE INGREDIENTS are new to you, be assured that you can find them in any city and in most decent suburban and even rural supermarkets. Though fish sauce may be an acquired taste, the only ingredient here that requires what might be an unfamiliar technique is whole lemongrass, which is usually sold by the stalk, looks like a scallion, and is easily handled. Sometimes supermarkets sell young or pre-trimmed lemongrass in packages; you can simply mince these with no prior preparation.

THE CUCUMBERS' JUICES are drawn out by salting, a process that takes some time but almost no effort. Just salt the seeded halves before slicing them to create firm but still quite moist slices that continue to weep and exude their liquid after slicing. This transforms a dressing that is already juicy—because it contains no oil, it has none of the body of a creamy vinaigrette—into one that is quite thin, an advantage in this instance.

Cucumber Salad with Shrimp: The easy way, and it's a good one, is simply to treat the shrimp exactly as you do the scallops; take about 1½ pounds shrimp (unpeeled are fine if you're willing to let your family or guests use their fingers at the table) and cook exactly as you do the scallops; shrimp are done when pink all over. Alternatively, peel the shrimp and marinate them for about 30 minutes in a mixture of 1 teaspoon minced garlic, 1 tablespoon coarse salt, ½ teaspoon cayenne, 1 teaspoon paprika, 2 tablespoons olive oil, and 2 teaspoons freshly squeezed lemon juice. Then cook and serve the shrimp as you would the scallops.

Cucumber Salad with Chicken: Marinate 1 to 1½ pounds boneless, skinless chicken breasts in a mixture of 2 tablespoons nam pla or soy sauce and 2 tablespoons lime juice while the cucumbers drain. Grill or broil the chicken until it is done, about 3 minutes per side. Cut into strips and serve as you would the scallops.

■ Toss a cup of washed, dried, and roughly chopped watercress, arugula, or spinach into the cucumbers before dressing.

■ Add a cup of peeled and minced apple, jicama, or minced bell pepper—preferably red or yellow, or a combination—to the cucumbers.

■ Slice a medium onion thinly, and separate it into rings. Salt the rings along with the cucumbers; their flavor will mellow considerably.

■ Increase the amount of herbs to one cup.

■ Toss a cup of bean sprouts into the salad.

Minty Broiled Shrimp Salad

TIME: 20 to 30 minutes

MAKES: 4 servings

The juices that foods exude as they're cooking are often lost in the shuffle, especially when that shuffle is grilling. When I was making this salad one time, however, it rained so hard I was forced to resort to the broiler. It was then I remembered why broiled shrimp are so desirable: You get to savor the delicious juices, the essences, produced by the shrimp themselves. (This is also true of shrimp that are sautéed or roasted or, for that matter, steamed in aluminum foil or poached in a stew.)

This newfound liquid and the time of year cried for a bed of greens. Not wanting to completely overwhelm delicately flavored greens with the powerfully spiced shrimp, I used a mixture of arugula, lettuce, and a high proportion of mint, dressed with olive oil and lemon juice. The result is a nice, juicy, big, flavorful—and easy—salad.

2 pounds shrimp in the 15-to-30-per-pound range, peeled (and deveined if you like)

1 teaspoon minced garlic or more to taste

1 teaspoon salt

½ teaspoon cayenne pepper, or to taste

1 teaspoon paprika

4 tablespoons olive oil

2 tablespoons plus 2 teaspoons fresh lemon juice

30 to 40 mint leaves

6 cups arugula and/or other greens

1 Preheat the broiler, and adjust the rack so that it is as close to the heat source as possible. Place a large ovenproof skillet or thick-bottomed roasting pan on the stove over low heat.

2 Combine the shrimp with the garlic, salt, cayenne, paprika, half the olive oil, and the 2 teaspoons lemon juice; stir to blend. Turn the heat under the skillet to high.

3 When the skillet smokes, toss in the shrimp. Shake the pan once or twice to distribute them evenly, then immediately place the skillet in the broiler.

4 Mince about one-third of the mint. Tear the remaining leaves and toss them with the arugula. Stir the remaining olive oil and lemon juice together in a bowl.

5 The shrimp are done when opaque; this will take only about 3 or 4 minutes. Use a slotted spoon to transfer the shrimp to a plate; it's fine if they cool for a moment. Add the shrimp juices to the olive oil-lemon juice mixture and stir. Dress the greens with this mixture and toss (if the greens seem dry, add a little more olive oil, lemon

WINE Any fresh, crisp, and inexpensive white, like Pinot Grigio or Muscadet.

SERVE WITH A true whole-meal dish, but one that certainly would not suffer from being served with a bit of crusty bread.

juice, or both). Place the greens on a platter and arrange the shrimp on top of or around them; garnish the shrimp with the minced mint.

Keys To SUCCESS

ALMOST ALL SHRIMP are frozen before sale. So unless you're in a hurry, you might as well buy them frozen and defrost them yourself; this will guarantee you that they are defrosted just before you cook them, therefore retaining peak quality.

THERE ARE NO UNIVERSAL STANDARDS for shrimp size; "large" and "medium" don't mean much. Therefore, it pays to learn to judge shrimp size by the number per pound, as retailers do. Shrimp labeled "16/20," for example, contain sixteen to twenty per pound; those labeled "U-20" require fewer (under) twenty to make a pound. Shrimp from fifteen to about thirty per pound usually give the best combination of flavor, ease (peeling tiny shrimp is a nuisance), and value (really big shrimp usually cost more than ten dollars a pound).

ON DEVEINING: I don't. You can, if you like, but it's a thankless task, and there isn't one person in a hundred who could blind-taste the difference between shrimp that have and have not been deveined.

Spicy Chicken Salad: This is better with boneless chicken thighs than breasts, but you can use either. Marinate and cook 1-inch chunks as you would the shrimp; they will take about the same amount of time. Remove the chicken, then place the pan over a burner; turn the heat to high and add ½ cup water. Stir and scrape to release any of the flavorful bits remaining in the pan (the chicken will not release as much liquid as the shrimp, which is why this step is necessary). When the liquid is reduced to a couple of tablespoons, combine it with the olive oil–lemon mixture and proceed as above.

■ There are many different directions in which you can take this dish. You can grill the shrimp instead of broiling them, and forget the salad. Their lively flavor and lovely color—contributed by the paprika—make them a great starter or finger food.

■ Use a combination of mint, cilantro, parsley, basil, and/or other aromatic herbs in place of mint alone. In fact, the herb component of this salad is infinitely variable. Use what you like, in any amounts and combinations you prefer.

■ Substitute sherry vinegar for lemon juice and add a teaspoon of cumin along with the paprika. Use chopped parsley in place of mint.

■ Use peanut oil in place of olive oil, lime juice in place of lemon juice, and cilantro in place of mint. Add a tablespoon or two of soy sauce or fish sauce (nam pla or nuoc mam) to the salad before tossing it.

LINGUINE WITH GARLIC AND OIL

PASTA WITH RED WINE SAUCE

PASTA WITH SAUSAGE

PASTA WITH MEATY BONES

ZITI WITH BUTTER, SAGE, AND PARMESAN

LINGUINE WITH SPINACH

SPAGHETTI WITH ZUCCHINI

SPAGHETTI WITH FRESH TOMATO SAUCE

ZITI WITH CHESTNUTS AND MUSHROOMS

PASTA WITH POTATOES

PENNE WITH BUTTERNUT SQUASH

RICE NOODLES WITH BASIL

PARMESAN CUPS WITH ORZO RISOTTO

Pasta

Linguine with Garlic and Oil

TIME: 30 minutes
MAKES: 4 servings

If you have a pantry, even a poorly stocked one, there is a good chance you can be eating this dish in twenty minutes. If your pantry is well stocked—for example, if you have some olives, capers, chickpeas, dried chiles, and so on—you can be making any of several variations, also in less than half an hour. All of these dishes, which are based on olive oil and little more, make great late-night snacks, light dinners or lunches, and fine first courses.

2 tablespoons minced garlic
½ cup extra virgin olive oil
Salt

1 pound linguine, spaghetti, or other long, thin pasta

1 Bring a large pot of water to a boil and salt it. Meanwhile, in a small skillet over medium-low heat, combine the garlic, oil, and a pinch of salt. Allow the garlic to simmer, shaking the pan occasionally, until it turns golden; do not allow it to become dark brown.

2 When the water boils, cook the pasta until it is tender but firm. When it is done, drain it, reserving a bit of the cooking water. Reheat the garlic and oil mixture briefly if necessary. Dress the pasta with the sauce, adding a little more oil or some of the cooking water if it seems dry.

WINE Crisp, dry white, like Orvieto, Pinot Grigio, or even Frascati.

SERVE WITH Great as a late-night snack, with nothing but a chunk of bread; salad (Grilled Bread Salad, page 24, would be perfect) or any vegetable would round out a meal.

SINCE OLIVE OIL is the backbone of this dish, use the best you can lay your hands on.

KEEP THE HEAT under the oil medium-low, because you want to avoid browning the garlic at all costs. (Well, not at all costs. If you brown the garlic, you'll have a different, more strongly flavored kind of dish, but one that is still worth eating.)

- Garnish with a good handful of chopped parsley. For 30 seconds' work, this makes an almost unbelievable difference.

- Add a couple of dried chiles to the oil along with the garlic. Discard the chiles before tossing the garlic-oil mixture with the pasta. Alternatively, sprinkle the pasta with crushed red pepper flakes, or pass some at the table.

- Add 1 cup cooked, drained chickpeas to the garlic-oil mixture about a minute before tossing with the pasta.

- Add 1 to 2 tablespoons capers to the garlic-oil mixture about a minute before tossing with the pasta.

- Add ¼ to ½ cup minced pitted black olives (preferably imported) to the garlic-oil mixture about a minute before tossing with the pasta.

- Add a mixture of about 1 cup fresh herbs to the pasta when tossing it with the garlic-oil mixture. You probably will need more olive oil or some of the pasta-cooking water.

Pasta with Red Wine Sauce

TIME: 30 minutes
MAKES: About 4 servings

Finishing pasta by cooking it for the final minute or two in stock is not all that uncommon. But simmering it in flavorful liquid for nearly all of its cooking time—almost as you would a risotto—is highly unusual. And when that liquid is red wine, the pasta is, well, unique. This dish was created by Alessandro Giuntoli, a Tuscan chef. It is in fact much better suited to home than restaurant cooking, because it must be prepared entirely at the last minute. It's simple enough, and there are aspects of it that are quite splendid: The pasta takes on a fruity acidity—smoothed by the last-minute addition of butter—and a beautiful mahogany glaze that's like nothing you've ever seen.

½ cup extra virgin olive oil
1 tablespoon minced garlic
1 teaspoon red pepper flakes, or to taste
Salt and freshly ground black pepper
1 pound spaghetti
1 bottle red wine, such as Chianti
1 tablespoon butter

1 Bring a large pot of water to a boil and salt it. Place the oil, garlic, and red pepper in a large, deep skillet.

2 When the water boils, add the pasta; turn the heat under the skillet to high. Cook the pasta as usual, stirring. As soon as the garlic begins to brown, sprinkle it with salt and pepper to taste and add three-fourths of the bottle of wine (a little more than 2 cups); bring to a boil and maintain it there.

3 When the pasta begins to bend—after less than 5 minutes of cooking—drain it and add it to the wine mixture. Cook, stirring occasionally, adding wine a little at a time if the mixture threatens to dry out completely.

4 Taste the pasta frequently. When it is done—tender but with a little bite—stir in the butter and turn off the heat. When the butter glazes the pasta, serve it immediately.

WINE A challenge; you can choose the same kind of wine that you use in the dish, but you're not going to want a lot of it. I'd drink water and save wine for the second course.

SERVE WITH This is a true starter, not a main course; follow it with something gutsy, like grilled meat or fish, or something grand like Crisp Roasted Rack of Lamb, page 146.

THE KIND OF WINE you use is of some importance, although it need not be expensive. Try a decent Chianti Classico, a light wine from the Côtes-du-Rhône, or a good (red) Zinfandel.

THE OTHER CRITICAL INGREDIENT is the pasta: For the timing to be precise, spaghetti works best here, producing the best texture.

■ You can easily add another dimension to this dish by tossing in about a cup of chopped walnuts—pieces of about ¼ inch, no smaller—along with the butter.

■ A garnish of chopped parsley or basil will make the presentation more attractive and the flavor somewhat brighter.

Pasta with Sausage

TIME: 30 minutes

MAKES: 4 to 6 servings

Most of us associate pasta and sausage with a dense, heavy tomato sauce, the kind that is so Italian-American it is just about indigenous. Yet sausage can contribute to a relatively light, almost delicate pasta sauce, especially if it is used in small amounts. In fact, sausage is the ideal meat to use in a quick pasta sauce, because it is preseasoned and cooks almost instantly.

1 tablespoon butter

½ pound sweet or hot Italian sausage, removed from the casing if necessary

½ cup water

1 pound ziti or other cut pasta

Salt and freshly ground black pepper

½ cup or more freshly grated Parmesan cheese

1 Bring a large pot of water to a boil for the pasta and salt it.

2 Place the butter in a medium skillet over medium-low heat. As it melts, crumble the sausage meat into it, making the bits quite small, ½ inch or less in size. Add the water and adjust the heat so that the mixture simmers gently.

3 Cook the pasta until it is tender but not at all mushy. Reserve about ½ cup of the cooking water.

4 Drain the pasta and dress with the sauce, adding some of the reserved cooking liquid if necessary. Add salt and pepper to taste. Toss with the Parmesan and serve.

WINE Powerful white, like a good Chardonnay, or light red, like Beaujolais or inexpensive Pinot Noir.

SERVE WITH This rich dish is best followed by or served with something light—salad or vegetables. You don't need much. Pear and Gorgonzola Green Salad, page 26, is ideal.

USE "ITALIAN" SAUSAGE, that which contains at least salt, pepper, fennel seeds, and other seasonings in small amounts; it can be hot if you like.

IF YOU CAN BUY sausage with no casing, so much the better; you're going to crumble it anyway.

White Pasta with Sausage and Onions: Before adding the sausage, gently cook about a cup of minced onion in the butter until it is translucent. Proceed as above.

Red Pasta with Sausage: Still far lighter than the pasta with sausage you're expecting. Cut up, seed, and drain 5 to 6 plum tomatoes; they may be fresh or canned. Add them to the sauce along with the sausage.

■ Add about a teaspoon of minced garlic or a couple of tablespoons of minced shallots to the butter as it melts.

■ Toss in a handful of chopped parsley or basil at the last moment, or add about a teaspoon of fresh thyme leaves or minced fresh sage along with the sausage.

■ Use red wine as the cooking liquid; its astringency offsets the sweet richness of butter and meat beautifully.

Pasta with Meaty Bones

TIME: At least 1 hour
MAKES: 4 to 6 servings

A basic tomato sauce is (or at least should be) a part of every cook's repertoire, since it's among the most fundamental dressings for pasta. Typically, you make this sauce by coloring a little garlic or onion in oil, then adding crushed tomatoes—in this instance canned are just about as good as fresh—and cooking them over medium-high heat. When the mixture becomes "saucy," about twenty minutes later, it's done.

The variations on this theme are nearly infinite. One of my favorites, which requires considerably more time but almost no extra effort, adds the wonderful depth of flavor, silken texture, and satisfying chewiness of slow-cooked meat. Southern Italian in origin, it begins with bony meat (or meaty bones) and requires lengthy simmering. Otherwise, it's little different from basic tomato sauce.

2 tablespoons olive oil

2 small dried hot red chiles, optional

1 piece meaty veal shank, ½ to 1 pound

3 garlic cloves, peeled and roughly chopped

Salt and freshly ground black pepper

One 28-ounce can whole plum tomatoes, with juice

1 pound ziti, penne, or other cut pasta

½ cup or more roughly chopped parsley or basil

1 Place the olive oil in a saucepan over medium heat. After a minute, add the optional chiles and cook for about 30 seconds. Add the veal shank and raise the heat to medium-high; cook, turning as necessary, until the meat is nicely browned, 10 minutes or more. When the meat is just about done, add the garlic and salt and pepper to taste.

2 When the garlic has softened a bit, crush the tomatoes and add them along with their juice. Turn the heat to medium-low to maintain a steady simmer. If you are using a broad pot, cover it partially. Cook, stirring occasionally, until the meat is tender and just about falling off the bone, at least 1 hour.

3 Bring a large pot of water to a boil and salt it. Cook the pasta until it is tender but firm. Remove the veal shank, scoop out any marrow, chop the meat coarsely, and return the meat to the sauce (discard the bone). Remove and discard the chiles.

4 Drain and sauce the pasta; sprinkle it with the herb, toss, and serve.

WINE Red and big: Barolo, Cabernet, or very good Zinfandel.
SERVE WITH Bread. You don't need anything else, but salad or a light vegetable dish (see Green Beans with Lemon, page 168) wouldn't hurt. Don't fuss, though.

WHATEVER YOU USE, the idea remains constant: Meat is a supporting player, not the star, so an eight- to twelve-ounce piece of veal shank, for example, provides enough meat, marrow, and gelatin to create a luxuriously rich sauce. Just cook until the meat falls off the bone, then chop it and return it to the sauce along with any marrow.

SIMPLE AS THIS IS, there are a couple of fine points: For best flavor, brown the meat well before adding the tomatoes. And use a narrow pot, because you don't want the sauce to become too thick during the relatively long cooking period; it's worth partially covering the pot as well.

THIS SAUCE IS RICH ENOUGH without grated cheese; a better garnish is a large handful of coarsely chopped parsley or basil. Either freshens the sauce while adding color and flavor.

Pasta with Ribs: This is one of the best ways to use a small amount of meat in a highly satisfying way. Substitute 6 to 8 meaty spareribs for the veal shank (you can even use a couple more). The cooking time may be a little shorter. Serve the pasta topped with sauce along with a couple of ribs on the side.

■ Carrots make a nice addition to this sauce; add about a cup, cut into chunks, along with the tomatoes. Some chopped onion won't do any harm either.

■ Use a ham hock or a big piece of bacon in place of some or all of the fresh meat.

■ You can use almost any bony meat you want here. Some of the best are: beef shin (it's the same cut as veal shank); oxtail, cut into sections; fresh ham hock; short ribs; veal ribs; or lamb shank.

Ziti with Butter, Sage, and Parmesan

TIME: 30 minutes
MAKES: 4 to 6 servings

The flour-enriched water in which pasta has cooked is never going to be an essential component of fine cooking, and it seldom appears in recipes. Yet from its origins as a cost-free, effortless substitute for stock, olive oil, butter, cream, or other occasionally scarce or even precious ingredients, pasta-cooking water has become a convenient and zero-calorie addition to simple sauces.

When you compare a lightly creamy sauce like the one in this recipe to the highly flavorful and ever-popular Alfredo sauce of butter, cream, eggs, and cheese, the latter seems relatively heavy. Substituting water for much of the butter and all of the cream and eggs produces a sauce with a perfect balance of weight and flavor. The water lends a quality not unlike that produced by tomatoes, as opposed to the slickness contributed by straight fat.

1 pound ziti, penne, or other
   cut pasta

2 tablespoons butter

30 fresh sage leaves

About 1 cup freshly grated
   Parmigiano-Reggiano

Salt and freshly ground black
   pepper

1 Bring a large pot of water to a boil and salt it. Cook the pasta until it is tender, but a little short of the point at which you want to eat it.

2 Meanwhile, place the butter in a skillet or saucepan large enough to hold the cooked pasta; turn the heat to medium and add the sage. Cook until the butter turns nut-brown and the sage shrivels, then turn the heat down to a minimum.

3 When the pasta is just about done, scoop out a cupful of the cooking water. Drain the pasta, immediately add it to the butter-sage mixture, and raise the heat to medium. Add ½ cup of the water and stir; the mixture will be loose and a little soupy. Cook for about 30 seconds, or until some of the water is absorbed and the pasta is perfectly done.

4 Stir in the cheese; the sauce will become creamy. Thin it with a little more water if necessary, season liberally with salt and pepper to taste, and serve immediately, passing more cheese at the table if you like.

WINE Almost any white, from a light one to a fine Chardonnay.

SERVE WITH This is best as a starter, not a main course, but it's still pretty rich. I would stick with a light fish preparation to follow—try Grilled Fish the Mediterranean Way, page 74, for example—or perhaps a big salad.

IN GENERAL, the water used to thin sauce need not come from cooking pasta; if you're making a sauce with vegetables such as broccoli or asparagus, that strongly flavored cooking liquid is another natural choice for the sauce base.

DON'T FORGET to reserve some of the pasta-cooking water before you drain the pasta! It's too late once it goes down the drain, as I've discovered several times . . .

- Fresh sage is the herb of choice here, but substitutions abound. Try parsley, thyme, chervil, or other green herbs in its place.

- Cook ¼ to ½ cup minced shallots or onions in the butter, just until they're translucent.

- Toast ½ cup bread crumbs or chopped nuts in the butter, just until they're lightly browned.

- Substitute extra virgin olive oil for some or all of the butter. The result will be good, if not as creamy.

Linguine with Spinach

TIME: 30 minutes
MAKES: 4 to 6 servings

Not long ago, it seemed that most cooks believed that the best pasta was topped with the most complex sauce imaginable. This led to improbable combinations such as penne with artichoke hearts, shrimp, goat cheese, pine nuts, sun-dried tomatoes, basil, cream, and Parmesan, which make bizarre, untraditional dishes.

The true nature of pasta is simplicity. I've long made a vegetable sauce by poaching greens such as spinach in the pasta water, then removing them and adding the pasta, a neat trick. But my friend Jack Bishop, author of *Vegetarian Italian Cooking*, went one step further, cooking the greens right in with the pasta.

The method relies on the fact that there is a range of doneness between the moment when the pasta's last traces of chalkiness disappear and it begins to become mushy, and this range lasts for two or three minutes. If, just before the pasta is done, you add the greens, whose tough stems have been removed, greens and pasta will finish cooking at the same time.

1 medium garlic clove

½ teaspoon red pepper flakes, or to taste, optional

¼ cup plus 1 tablespoon extra virgin olive oil

1 pound linguine or other long pasta

1 pound spinach, washed, tough stems removed, roughly chopped

Salt and freshly ground black pepper

1 Bring a large pot of water to a boil and salt it. Meanwhile, mince the garlic as finely as possible and combine it in the bottom of a warm bowl with the red pepper and olive oil.

2 Add the pasta to the pot and cook until it is nearly done (test it for doneness by tasting). Plunge the spinach into the water and cook until it wilts, less than a minute. Drain quickly, allowing some water to cling to the pasta, and toss in the bowl with the garlic and olive oil mixture. Season with salt and pepper to taste and serve.

WINE Spinach can be a wine-killer, so stick with something simple and cool, like a crisp white or a lightly chilled Beaujolais or Chianti.

SERVE WITH Close to a one-dish meal; just add bread and call it done.

WHEN MAKING THIS DISH and others like it, you must adhere to the often ignored canon of allowing at least a gallon of water per pound of pasta, because you need a pot large enough to accommodate the greens, and because they cannot be allowed to slow down the cooking too much.

WHILE THE PASTA COOKS, mix the seasonings in a warm bowl. The sauce is finished by the spinach and the moisture retained by it and the pasta itself.

ALTHOUGH THERE IS NO "CORRECT" MOMENT to add the vegetable, I suggest that you add tender greens such as spinach when the pasta is just about done, since the additional cooking time is only going to be another thirty seconds or so. Add tougher greens, such as kale or collards—or vegetables like broccoli florets—a minute or two before you judge the pasta to be finished, so that the greens have enough time to become tender.

One-Pot Pasta and Greens, Asian Style: Use Asian wheat noodles, and substitute ¼ cup peanut oil plus 1 tablespoon sesame oil for the olive oil. Add 1 tablespoon soy sauce to the hot pepper and garlic; garnish with 2 tablespoons lightly toasted sesame seeds.

■ Toss the pasta with freshly grated Parmesan or pecorino cheese to taste.

■ Add any of the following to the garlic-pepper-oil mixture, singly or in combination: about 15 calamata or other olives, pitted and roughly chopped; about ¼ cup chopped sun-dried tomatoes packed in oil; about 2 tablespoons drained capers; about ½ cup toasted bread crumbs; about ¼ cup minced prosciutto or other dry-cured ham.

■ Use other greens; as long as they will cook quickly, they'll be fine. Try the chopped leaves of kale, collards, Swiss chard, turnip or mustard greens, or Chinese cabbage, or bite-sized florets of broccoli or cauliflower.

Spaghetti with Zucchini

This dish—which has zucchini as its focus—is simply amazing when made in midsummer with tender, crisp squash, but it isn't half-bad even when made in midwinter with a limp vegetable that's traveled halfway around the world to get to your table. Either way, it is an unusual use for zucchini, which here substitutes for meat in a kind of vegetarian spaghetti carbonara, the rich pasta dish featuring eggs, bacon, and Parmesan. Made with zucchini instead of bacon, obviously, the dish becomes a little less fat-laden, but it is still rich and delicious.

3 tablespoons olive oil

3 or 4 small zucchini (about 1 pound), washed, trimmed, and cut into slices ⅛ to ¼ inch thick

Salt and freshly ground black pepper

2 eggs

1 cup freshly grated Parmesan cheese

1 pound spaghetti, linguine, or other long pasta

½ cup roughly chopped mint, parsley, or basil

1 Put a large pot of water to boil over high heat and salt it. Place the olive oil in a 10- or 12-inch skillet over medium-high heat. A minute later, add the zucchini; cook, stirring only occasionally, until very tender and lightly browned, 10 to 15 minutes. Season with a little salt and a lot of pepper.

2 Meanwhile, beat the eggs and ½ cup of the Parmesan together. Add the pasta to the boiling water and cook until it is tender but firm. When it is done, drain it and combine it immediately with the egg-cheese mixture, tossing until the egg appears cooked. Stir in the zucchini, then taste and add more salt and pepper if necessary.

3 Toss in the herb and serve immediately, passing the remaining Parmesan at the table.

WINE Good, rich Chardonnay.
SERVE WITH Bread and salad will do it.

BE SURE TO COOK THE ZUCCHINI long enough to brown it a bit, which will enhance its flavor.

THE EGGS WILL COOK FULLY from the heat of the pasta. If this makes you at all nervous, however, do the final tossing of eggs, cheese, and pasta in the cooking pot, over the lowest flame possible.

USE TOP-QUALITY HARD CHEESE HERE, since its flavor will dominate. Genuine Parmigiano-Reggiano is best, but a good hard pecorino is also nice.

THE DISTINCTIVELY FRESH TASTE OF MINT is the most unusual aspect of this preparation, but you can certainly substitute basil or parsley.

Spaghetti Carbonara: The classic. Substitute ½ to 1 cup chopped bacon (preferably from a slab) or pancetta for the zucchini. When crisp, remove with a slotted spoon and drain on paper towels. It's traditional, but not essential, to use some of the cooking fat in the sauce. Garnish with parsley (or not at all).

Fettuccine Alfredo: Omit the zucchini. Just toss the pasta (preferably fettuccine) with eggs, cheese, and enough heavy cream to bind the sauce. Best served as a small first course for 6 to 8.

Spaghetti with Fresh Tomato Sauce

TIME: 20 minutes
MAKES: 4 to 6 servings

If you believe that timing is everything, this is the dish for you. You can only make it for part of the year, and you must seize the right moment to stop cooking the sauce—which happens to be a mere ten minutes or so after you begin. The dish has a thick creaminess that you can never duplicate with canned tomatoes, no matter how good they are. So the season is fairly short—where I live, just two or at the most three months a year.

3 tablespoons butter or olive oil

1½ to 2 pounds fresh tomatoes (preferably plum), cored and roughly chopped

1 pound spaghetti, linguine, or other long pasta

½ cup freshly grated Parmigiano-Reggiano

Salt and freshly ground black pepper

1 Bring a large pot of water to a boil and salt it. Place the butter or oil in an 8- or 10-inch skillet and turn the heat to medium. When the butter melts or the oil is hot, add the tomatoes and turn the heat to high.

2 Cook, stirring occasionally, until the tomatoes begin to juice up, then turn the heat to low and cook, stirring occasionally, until the sauce thickens.

3 Cook the pasta until it is tender but firm. Drain and toss with the tomatoes and cheese. Season with salt and pepper to taste, toss again, and serve immediately.

WINE A wide range of wines will work here, but I prefer good whites; Pinot Blanc is nice, or a good Chardonnay.

SERVE WITH This is good as a starter, followed by grilled meat, fish, and/or vegetables. Or you can serve bigger portions with a salad and bread.

FRESH TOMATOES should always be cored before using them (remove a cone-shaped wedge from the stem end). Peeling is optional—if you object to little bits of skin in your sauce, it's worth the effort. Just drop the tomatoes into boiling water for ten seconds, remove with a slotted spoon, and slip the peel right off. (Alternately, you can also fish out the skin as the sauce simmers; it automatically separates from the flesh.)

THERE IS AN IDEAL INSTANT for serving this sauce: When the tomatoes soften and all of their juices are in the skillet, the sauce suddenly begins to thicken. At that moment, it is at its peak; another minute or two later, many of the juices have evaporated and, although the essence of the sauce is equally intense, it doesn't coat the pasta as well. If this happens, just add a little fresh olive oil or butter to the finished dish.

- Add about a teaspoon of minced garlic to the butter or oil, just before the tomatoes. Garnish with minced parsley instead of Parmesan.

- Add about a tablespoon of minced shallot to the butter or oil.

- Cook the tomatoes with a couple of branches of basil, remove them before serving, and stir about ½ cup or more of roughly chopped basil leaves into the pasta.

- Toss the pasta with about a cup of cubed (½ inch or less) mozzarella, preferably fresh.

- Add crushed red pepper flakes to taste along with the tomatoes.

Ziti with Chestnuts and Mushrooms

TIME: 30 minutes
MAKES: 4 to 6 servings

Chestnuts and dried mushrooms have a wonderful affinity for one another. Their unusual flavors and textures seem distantly related; they are both meaty and complex, chewy but neither tough nor crunchy. With shallots and plenty of black pepper for bite, the combination makes a great pasta sauce.

And though chestnuts are a pain in the neck (the fingers, actually) to peel, the good news is that their complex, fragrant flavor is so powerfully distinctive that just a few can have an enormous impact on a dish. So although it may take thirty seconds to a minute to process a single chestnut, if you only need a dozen or so for a dish, the work amounts to about ten minutes. And in a creation like the one here, the time is well worth the effort.

15 chestnuts

1 ounce dried mushrooms— porcini, shiitake, black trumpets, morels, or an assortment

3 tablespoons butter or extra virgin olive oil

½ cup peeled and sliced shallots

Salt and freshly ground black pepper

1 pound ziti or other cut pasta

1 Cut a ring around each chestnut, then place them in boiling water to cover and cook for 3 minutes. Remove them from the water, a few at a time, and peel while still hot. Meanwhile, soak the mushrooms in about 1½ cups very hot water.

2 Bring a large pot of water to a boil and salt it. Place half the butter or oil in a skillet, turn the heat to medium-high and, a minute later, add the shallots. Sprinkle lightly with salt to taste and cook, stirring, until softened, 3 to 5 minutes. Chop the chestnuts into ½- to ¼-inch chunks, then measure about 1 cup. Add them to the skillet, along with a little more salt.

3 Cook, stirring occasionally, until the chestnuts deepen in color, about 5 minutes. Remove the mushrooms from their soaking liquid; strain, reserving the liquid. Chop the mushrooms and add them to the skillet; cook, stirring, for a minute or two, then add the strained mushroom-soaking liquid. Turn the heat to low and season to taste with salt and lots of black pepper.

WINE A rich dish that will stand up to a good red—nothing lighter than Zinfandel, and Cabernet would not be out of place.

SERVE WITH This can serve as a main course, and you don't need a lot else with it—some steamed broccoli, or a salad, and some bread. If you want to do a little work, Beet Roesti with Rosemary, page 170, would be a rewarding choice.

4 Cook the pasta until tender but not mushy. If the sauce is too thick, add a little of the pasta-cooking water to it when the pasta is nearly done. Stir in the remaining butter or oil, then drain the pasta and dress with the sauce. Serve immediately.

Keys To SUCCESS

THERE ARE MANY WAYS to peel chestnuts, which like most nuts have a hard outer shell and a soft inner skin. Removing them both is a three-step process. First, use a paring knife—a curved one with a sharp point makes this quick and easy—to cut a ring around the equator of each nut or make an "X" on the flat side. Plunge the nuts into boiling water to cover for about three minutes, then turn off the heat, leaving the chestnuts in the water. Remove two or three at a time and, using the knife and your fingers, peel off both shell and skin; use a towel to protect your hands from the heat if necessary. If you're doing a large batch— say, twenty or more—you'll notice that as the water cools the skins become more difficult to remove. Bring the pot back to a boil and they'll begin to slip off again.

ALTHOUGH THE EXACT COUNT OF CHESTNUTS for this dish is not critical, I begin with fifteen, because there are usually a couple of rotten ones, or some whose inner skin refuses to come off. These must be discarded.

With MINIMAL Effort

Ziti with Chestnuts and Fresh Mushrooms: You'll need about 8 ounces fresh mushrooms, trimmed and chopped (again, an assortment is best); 1 to 1½ cups chicken or other stock; and a few more minutes. Steps 1 and 2 remain the same; in Step 3, add the mushrooms before the chestnuts, and cook, stirring, until they become tender, about 5 minutes; then add the chestnuts and cook, stirring, another 5 minutes. Add 1 cup of the chicken stock and cook until the chestnuts are tender and the mixture "saucy," about 10 minutes, adding a little more stock if necessary.

■ Combine fresh and reconstituted dried mushrooms—first cook the fresh until soft, then add the dried. Proceed as in the variation above.

■ Add a few sprigs of fresh thyme along with the shallots. Remove before serving, and sprinkle fresh thyme leaves as a garnish.

■ Add diced (¼ inch or less) zucchini; peeled, seeded, and diced tomato; or red bell pepper— no more than a cup total—along with the chestnuts.

Pasta with Potatoes

TIME: 60 minutes

MAKES: At least 8 servings

This is about as unlikely a dish as I've ever come across, a soupy combination containing little more than the two main ingredients and canned tomatoes. Not only does the thought of it tweak the mind—doesn't this sound something like a bread sandwich?—but it counters a number of the conventions that have been drummed into our collective consciousness.

Chief among these is that the dish is at its best when the pasta is cooked until it is fat, juice-laden, and quite soft. Here, there is no need to seize the ideal moment at which the pasta is al dente; in fact, you cook the pasta somewhat past that point, and it is even acceptable for it to sit for a while. Nor need you worry about the "correct" pasta shape; pasta with potatoes requires several different shapes, in varying quantities, preferably broken (it began as a way to use up the bits and pieces of dried pasta lying around in the cupboard). Finally, not only may you serve pasta with potatoes as a leftover, it's just as good after sitting for a day.

2 tablespoons olive oil

About ½ cup minced pancetta or bacon, optional

3 to 4 potatoes (about 1½ pounds), peeled and cut into bite-sized chunks

1 tablespoon chopped garlic

3 to 4 small dried hot red chiles (or about 1 teaspoon crushed red pepper flakes), or to taste

One 28-ounce can whole plum tomatoes, with juice

About 1½ pounds assorted leftover dried pasta

Salt and freshly ground black pepper

Several cups of water, kept at a simmer in a pot or kettle

1 Place the olive oil in a large saucepan and turn the heat to medium. If you're using pancetta or bacon, add it to the oil and cook, stirring occasionally, until it becomes slightly crisp, about 10 minutes. (If you are omitting the meat, proceed to the next step.)

2 Add the potatoes, garlic, and chiles, and raise the heat to medium-high. Cook, stirring occasionally, until the potatoes begin to brown all over, about 10 minutes.

3 Add the tomatoes and their juice, along with 2 cups water, and bring to a boil. Turn the heat down to medium-low and cook, uncovered, stirring occasionally to break up the tomatoes and prevent sticking.

4 While the potatoes are cooking, break long pasta, such as spaghetti, into several lengths; place cut pasta, such as ziti, in a bag and smack it into pieces with the back of a pot or a hammer. After the potatoes have simmered for about 10 minutes, add the pasta and plenty of salt and pepper to the pot. Simmer, stirring and adding water as

WINE This is a peasant dish, so you need a rough red, like Chianti.

SERVE WITH Very simple: bread, and salad if you like.

necessary—the mixture should remain thick and stewy, never dry.

5 When the potatoes and pasta are both quite tender—this will take 20 minutes or more—the dish is done. (It may be covered and refrigerated for a day or two, or put in a closed container and frozen for several weeks; it's likely that you will need to add more liquid when you reheat it.) Check the seasoning and add some crushed red pepper flakes, black pepper, and/or salt if needed. Serve hot, in bowls.

Pasta and Potato Soup: This dish is a stew, and like most stews it can readily be converted to soup: Add 2 to 4 cups water (or, even better, chicken stock) in Step 5. Heat and serve with a spoon.

■ After the potatoes begin to brown, add 1 to 2 cups chopped onions and cook, stirring, until they soften before proceeding.

■ Add small bits of cooked or raw meat—up to 2 cups—along with the potatoes.

■ Add chunks of carrots and/or celery—up to 2 cups—along with the potatoes.

■ Cook a few stems of basil in the stew. Remove before serving, then garnish with plenty of chopped fresh basil.

■ Serve with freshly grated pecorino or Parmesan cheese.

Keys To SUCCESS

MOST PASTA LOVERS have a few open boxes in their cabinets, but if you must make this with only one shape of pasta, that's no crime—it'll just be somewhat less enchanting.

PASTA WITH POTATOES is very kid-friendly, with much of the appeal of alphabet soup or even Chef Boyardee. For that reason, you might consider cooking it without chiles and passing crushed red pepper at the table, so adults can add some assertiveness to this somewhat bland dish while kids eat it as is.

BE CAREFUL NOT TO COOK the dish too dry. If, at the last minute, the pasta has absorbed nearly all the liquid, stir in another cup or so of water and cook for a minute or two longer.

Penne with Butternut Squash

Go to central or Northern Italy in autumn and you're sure to be offered tortelli or other pasta filled with zucca, a pumpkin-like vegetable whose flesh, like that of butternut or acorn squash, is dense, orange, and somewhat sweet. To make a pasta filling, zucca is cooked and pureed with nutmeg, eggs, and Parmesan cheese.

The resulting tortelli, normally bathed in butter and grated Parmesan, are unforgettably delicious. The rub is that making them is a serious project, beginning with making and rolling out fresh pasta dough and ending with cutting, stuffing, and sealing the individual tortelli. Because preparing the stuffing is simplicity itself, however, the flavor and essential nature of pasta with zucca can be captured in a thirty-minute preparation that is admittedly a compromise, but a very good one. What you do is prepare the zucca in a thin version, so the stuffing becomes a sauce. The result is inside out, and not as attractive as tortelli, but the flavor and texture are right there.

1 pound peeled and seeded butternut squash (start with a whole squash weighing about 1½ pounds)

2 tablespoons butter or olive oil

Salt and freshly ground black pepper

1 pound penne or other cut pasta

⅛ teaspoon freshly grated nutmeg, or to taste

1 teaspoon sugar, optional

½ cup freshly grated Parmesan cheese

1 Cut the squash into chunks and place it in a food processor. Pulse the machine on and off until the squash appears grated. Alternatively, grate or chop the squash by hand. Set a large pot of salted water to boil for the pasta.

2 Place a large skillet over medium heat and add the butter or oil. A minute later, add the squash, salt and pepper to taste, and about ½ cup water. Cook over medium heat, stirring occasionally. Add water, about ¼ cup at a time, as the mixture dries out, but be careful not to make it soupy. When the squash begins to disintegrate, after about 10 to 15 minutes, begin cooking the pasta. While it cooks, season the squash with the nutmeg, sugar if necessary, and additional salt and pepper if needed.

3 When the pasta is tender, scoop out about ½ cup of the cooking liquid and reserve it, then drain the pasta. Toss the pasta in the skillet with the squash, adding the reserved pasta-cooking water if the mixture seems dry. Taste and add more of any seasonings you like, then toss with the Parmesan and serve.

WINE Light red, like Chianti or Beaujolais.

SERVE WITH Best as a starter, followed by roast poultry or some other hearty, simple main course (this is a good place for Roast Pork with Applesauce, page 156).

PEEL THE SQUASH WITH A KNIFE, not a vegetable peeler, which is likely to break. And don't worry if you take a bunch of the flesh along with the peel; remember that the squash probably cost all of twenty-nine cents a pound.

SOME BUTTERNUT SQUASH is sweeter than others, and there's no way to predict this by appearance. Since this sauce relies on sweetness for its character, if the squash seems a little bland as it cooks, add about a teaspoon of sugar. It will brighten the flavor considerably.

■ Substitute 1 teaspoon minced garlic or 2 tablespoons minced shallot or onion for the nutmeg.

■ Garnish with a handful of chopped fresh herbs—parsley is a natural, but basil or chervil would also be good. Or add a few leaves of minced sage in Step 2 (omit the nutmeg).

■ Finish the dish with ½ cup of sweet cream, sour cream, or crème fraîche in place of the pasta-cooking water.

■ Cook about ½ pound of crumbled ground meat (beef, pork, chicken, or turkey) along with the squash.

Rice Noodles with Basil

TIME: 40 minutes

MAKES: 4 servings

Asians use wheat and rice noodles with equal frequency—but not interchangeably. In fact, rice noodles look different, require different handling, and taste different from wheat pasta.

For one thing, they're stark white. For another, they're best when soaked for a few minutes in hot water, then boiled just until their raw flavor disappears. Finally, they're never really what you call al dente, but rather quite soft. Here, they're stir-fried with basil, to create a basic, simple rice noodle dish that's easy to expand on.

12 ounces rice stick noodles

2 tablespoons peanut or vegetable oil

1 tablespoon minced garlic

1 teaspoon minced fresh hot chiles or crushed red pepper flakes, or to taste

1 teaspoon sugar

Salt and freshly ground black pepper

2 tablespoons nam pla (fish sauce) or soy sauce, or to taste

1 tablespoon lime juice, or to taste

½ cup roughly chopped Thai or other basil or mint

1 Soak the rice noodles in hot water to cover for 15 to 30 minutes, changing the water once or twice if possible. (If you change the water a couple of times the noodles will soften faster.) Meanwhile, bring a pot of water to a boil. When the noodles are soft, drain them, then immerse them in the boiling water for about 30 seconds. Drain and rinse in cold water.

2 Heat the oil in a deep skillet (preferably nonstick) over medium-high heat. Add the garlic and chiles and cook for about 30 seconds, stirring. Raise the heat to high, then add the noodles and sugar and toss to blend. Season with salt and pepper to taste.

3 When the noodles are hot, add the nam pla and lime juice. Taste and adjust seasoning as necessary, then stir in the basil or mint and serve.

WINE Beer is the best choice.

SERVE WITH Follow or serve with stir-fried vegetables or a meat- or fish-and-vegetable stir-fry. Shrimp in Yellow Curry, page 94, or Chicken with Coconut and Lime, page 116, would each make a feast out of this.

YOU MIGHT SEE fresh rice noodles from time to time, but for the most part they are sold dried, like most pasta, only in far fewer shapes, ranging from very thin to linguinelike to fettuccinelike; that's about it. The superthin ones (usually called vermicelli) are best for soups. The two thicker varieties, usually called rice sticks, are best for stir-fries like this one.

IN A STIR-FRY LIKE THIS, you can get away with simply soaking the noodles, but I believe there's a little improvement in boiling the noodles for 30 seconds or so after soaking. Try it and see.

SUBSTITUTE SOY SAUCE for the nam pla if you like. Thai basil, which looks different from regular basil, can be found in many Asian markets; it's fabulously fragrant.

Pad Thai: It's not a far cry from this dish to the ever-popular pad Thai, which takes a little more effort, but not much. In Step 2, add about 1 cup medium shrimp, peeled; stir for a minute, then add 2 lightly beaten eggs. Let set for a few seconds, then scramble the eggs. Add the noodles, sugar, salt, pepper, nam pla, and lime juice as above. Garnish with about a cup of mung bean sprouts, ½ cup chopped salted peanuts, and basil (or cilantro). Serve with lime quarters.

■ Before adding the garlic, quickly stir-fry about 1 cup of ground or chopped pork, beef, chicken, or turkey until the color is gone. Proceed as above.

■ Before adding the garlic, stir-fry 1 to 2 cups of tender shredded vegetables, such as leeks, cabbage, Chinese cabbage (like bok choy), celery, bean sprouts, sliced mushrooms, or a combination. Proceed as above.

■ Add about a tablespoon of curry powder to the oil along with the garlic. Add more to taste if desired. Proceed as above.

Parmesan Cups
with Orzo Risotto

TIME: 30 minutes
MAKES: 4 servings

A couple of years ago, on a trip to central Italy—where true Parmigiano-Reggiano is made—I learned yet another use for the world's most important cheese. A cook in a trattoria was taking handfuls of the grated stuff, sprinkling them in a skillet, and forming melted cheese pancakes. While they were still warm, he draped them over the back of a cup to form crisp, edible, single-ingredient containers. He filled these with a mixture of zucchini, eggplant, and tomatoes, and sent them out as a first course.

I found the idea intriguing, but not all that easy to duplicate at home, where my skillet seemed always too hot or too cool, the pancakes too thick or too thin. But when I took the task seriously and set about figuring out the most reliable way to produce these Parmesan cups, it turned out to be fairly straightforward. Thanks to the miracle of the nonstick surface, just place four rounds of grated cheese on a baking sheet and, five minutes later, they're done.

2 cups good chicken or other stock

1 cup orzo (rice-shaped pasta)

1 cup freshly grated Parmesan cheese (about ¼ pound)

Salt and freshly ground black pepper

½ cup minced parsley leaves

1 Preheat the oven to 350°F.

2 Bring the stock to a boil in a 6- to 8-cup saucepan; stir in the orzo, cover, and turn the heat to medium-low. Set a timer for 15 minutes.

3 Use a ¼-cup measure to make 4 rounds of Parmesan on a nonstick baking sheet. Smooth the rounds into thin pancakes, 5 or 6 inches across; the thickness need not be perfectly uniform. Place the baking sheet in the oven.

4 The Parmesan rounds are done when the centers darken slightly and the edges begin to brown, about 5 to 6 minutes. Remove the baking sheet from the oven and let it stand for about a minute, then carefully lift each of the rounds and drape it over the bottom of a narrow cup or glass to form a cup shape. Let dry for about 5 minutes.

5 The orzo is done when it is tender and all the liquid has been absorbed, about 15 minutes. Season it with pepper and very little salt, then stir in the parsley. Spoon a portion of orzo into each of the Parmesan cups and serve.

WINE You can break out a good red here, like Cabernet or Pinot Noir.

SERVE WITH An elegant but filling starter like this should be followed by something simple, perhaps broiled or grilled fish—Striped Bass with Mushrooms, for example, page 76—and a salad.

BE CAREFUL NOT TO GRATE the cheese too finely; you don't want the same powdery consistency you might prefer on pasta. One of the larger holes of a box grater works well, and so does the steel blade of the food processor, which produces small, even pellets of cheese.

BAKING THE CHEESE DISKS doesn't present much of a problem, and it's easy enough to tell when they're done because the edges begin to brown. But removing them from the baking sheet can be tricky: Make sure to allow the rounds to cool slightly so that they can firm up a bit—thirty to sixty seconds is right for me, but if your baking sheet retains more heat it might take a little longer—and then use the thinnest spatula you have to lift them gently off the baking sheet. Drape the soft mass over a narrow glass, and shape gently; the cups will be ready to fill in a few minutes.

ALTHOUGH THEY'RE BEST WHEN FRESH, these will retain both shape and flavor for a couple of hours.

Cheese cups can be made with almost any hard cheese, or a combination of cheeses. Manchego, pecorino, and other sheep's milk cheeses are especially good.

As for fillings, try:

- Steamed and chopped spinach (other than some freshly ground pepper, no seasoning is necessary)
- Beef stew or other stewed meat
- Ratatouille or other stewed vegetables

EMMA'S COD AND POTATOES

ROAST COD WITH TANGERINE SAUCE

COD CAKES WITH GINGER AND SCALLIONS

FLOUNDER POACHED IN BROTH

SPARKLING CIDER–POACHED FISH

GRILLED FISH THE MEDITERRANEAN WAY

STRIPED BASS WITH MUSHROOMS

GRILLED TUNA WITH MESCLUN STUFFING

SEARED SALMON FILLETS

SALMON BURGERS

GRAVLAX

GRILLED OR BROILED LOBSTER

MUSSELS, ASIAN STYLE

PAELLA, FAST AND EASY

Fish
and Shellfish

SHRIMP WITH LEMONGRASS

SHRIMP IN YELLOW CURRY

STUFFED SCALLOPS

Emma's Cod and Potatoes

TIME: 1 hour
MAKES: 4 servings

Once, for a special occasion, I produced potatoes Anna for my daughter Emma, a dish in which potatoes are thin-sliced, drenched in butter, and roasted until golden—the ultimate in crisp potato dishes. This was a fatal error, because potatoes Anna are a pain to make, contain about a week's allotment of butter, and were forever in demand thereafter.

So I set about not only shortcutting the process, but also creating something approaching an entire meal. I cut back on the butter (when attacks of conscience strike I substitute olive oil) and enlisted the aid of the broiler in speeding the browning process. I figured that it would be just as easy to broil something on top of the potatoes during the last few minutes of cooking and, after a few tries, I found a thick fillet of fish to be ideal. The result is this simple weeknight dish that I now make routinely, and one that even impresses guests.

4 to 5 medium potatoes, 2 pounds or more

6 tablespoons extra virgin olive oil or melted butter

Salt and freshly ground black pepper

1½ pounds cod or other fillets, about 1 inch thick (skinned), in 2 or more pieces

1 Preheat the oven to 400°F. Peel the potatoes and cut them into slices about ⅛ inch thick (a mandoline comes in handy here). Toss the potatoes in an 8 × 11-inch or similar size baking pan with 4 tablespoons of the oil or butter. Season the potatoes liberally with salt and pepper, spread them evenly, and place the pan in the oven.

2 Cook for about 40 minutes, checking once or twice, until the potatoes are tender when pierced with a thin-bladed knife and have begun to brown on top. Turn on the broiler and adjust the rack so that it is 4 to 6 inches from the heat source.

3 Top the potatoes with the fish, drizzle with the remaining oil or butter, and sprinkle with some more salt and pepper. Broil until the fish is done, 6 to 10 minutes depending on its thickness (a thin-bladed knife will pass through it easily). If at any point the top of the potatoes begins to burn, move the pan a couple of inches farther away from the heat source.

WINE A rich, full-bodied Chardonnay would cut it, or you could go with a light, fruity red, but a semi-serious one, like Pinot Noir.

SERVE WITH This is close to a meal in itself; add a salad or a vegetable (try Roasted Asparagus with Parmesan, page 166) and you're set.

COOKING TIME IS DETERMINED by thickness, both of the potato slices and the fish. If you have a mandoline (or a sharp knife and good cutting skills), aim for slicing the potatoes about an eighth of an inch thick—this will allow them to cook through and begin to brown within forty minutes or so.

THE COD OR OTHER FISH should be about an inch thick; during the eight or so minutes it takes to cook through, the tops of the exposed potatoes will gain a fine crust, while the fish browns lightly.

- Toss 1 teaspoon or more of minced garlic with the potatoes.

- Mix up to ½ cup chopped parsley, dill, basil, or chervil, or smaller amounts (1 or 2 teaspoons) of stronger herbs like thyme or rosemary with the potatoes.

- Season the potatoes with a tablespoon or so of curry, chili powder, or paprika, or a few pinches of cayenne or crushed red pepper flakes.

- Top the fish with thin-sliced tomatoes and drizzle them with olive oil or dot them with butter before broiling.

- Add other vegetables to the potatoes—a cup or more of chopped spinach, for example—but be aware that their moisture may keep the potatoes from browning well.

Roast Cod with Tangerine Sauce

TIME: 30 minutes
MAKES: 4 servings

Nearly everyone likes the taste of tangerine, yet it remains rare in cooking, probably because it is easily overwhelmed. Here, however, is a sauce that preserves the fresh and distinctive flavor of the fruit and also has substance. It's delicate and best suited to a piece of fish, and a mild-flavored one at that. But it's equally good with chicken and—while it doesn't stand out as much—it is not bad with duck or pork.

4 to 5 large tangerines, at least 1½ pounds

1 tablespoon olive oil

1½ pounds cod or other mild white fish

Salt

Cayenne pepper

2 tablespoons butter or olive oil

1 Preheat the oven to 500°F; if you have a baking stone, use it. Finely grate the zest of the tangerines, avoiding grating any of the bitter white part (you should be able to get away with one swipe per section of skin on a good grater, rather than rubbing over and over). Set the zest aside. Juice the tangerines and measure 1¼ cups of the juice. Set the juice in a small saucepan over medium-high heat, bring to a boil, and reduce, stirring occasionally, to about ½ cup; this will take at least 10 minutes.

2 Place a large, ovenproof skillet, preferably nonstick, over high heat and add the oil. If necessary, cut the cod into serving pieces so that it will fit in the skillet comfortably. When the oil smokes, pour out any excess (you only need a film of oil). Add the fish and put the skillet in the oven; set a timer for 6 minutes.

3 When the timer goes off, check the fish; it is done when it offers no resistance to a thin-bladed knife and is opaque, or nearly so, throughout. Unless it is unusually thick, it will be done in no more than 8 minutes.

WINE Red, and not too too light; a minor Cabernet would not be out of place.

SERVE WITH White rice is almost a must; the juices of the fish or meat mingle with the tangerine sauce in a way that makes the rice heavenly. Any cooked green vegetable would complete the picture; Tender Spinach, Crisp Shallots, page 174, would be especially fine.

4 While the fish is cooking, season the tangerine sauce with salt and cayenne to taste—it should have something of a bite. Whisk in the butter or oil, a little at a time, until the sauce is smooth and thick; taste and adjust seasoning, then add the grated zest; cook another 15 seconds. Serve the fish napped with the sauce.

Roast Chicken with Tangerine Sauce: Use bone-in or boneless breasts, and broil them. For bone-in, set the rack 4 to 6 inches from the heat source, sprinkle the breasts (4 halves for 4 people) with salt and pepper, and rub with olive oil or butter. Broil, turning frequently, until nicely browned and cooked through, 10 to 15 minutes. For boneless, set the rack 4 inches or closer to the heat source; sprinkle the breasts (4 halves for 4 people) with salt and pepper, and rub with olive oil or butter. Broil without turning until cooked through, about 6 minutes.

■ Add a teaspoon of coriander seeds to the sauce as it reduces. These add a mysterious if mild flavor and a tiny bit of crunch.

■ Different herbs change the character of the sauce in different ways, even when added as a simple garnish. A tablespoon or two of minced dill accentuates the sweetness of the tangerine; a quarter-cup of chopped parsley leaves offsets it with bitterness; and a couple of tablespoons of chopped cilantro leaves (especially if there are coriander seeds in the sauce) makes the preparation seem exotic.

Keys To SUCCESS

IF YOU'VE NEVER "REDUCED" A LIQUID, don't be worried: It means nothing more than boiling out some of the water to intensify the essential flavors. (See page 188 for a fuller description of the process.)

COOKING TANGERINE JUICE flattens out its flavor, so a bit of fresh, uncooked tangerine zest is stirred in at the end of cooking to restore brightness.

Cod Cakes with Ginger and Scallions

TIME: 1 hour
MAKES: 4 servings

Between your favorite crabcake and a box of frozen fish sticks lies a world of crisp, easily produced fish cakes that make for great weeknight eating. In addition to fish, they all have two elements in common: something to "bind" the cake as it cooks, and a fair amount of seasoning.

My favorite way to hold fish cakes together is to mix the flaked meat with mashed potatoes, in a proportion of about three parts fish to one part potato. If you begin with a mild fish, such as cod, the flavorings can be as adventuresome as you like. My preferred combination is a hefty dose of ginger and cilantro, spiked with a bit of hot red pepper. The result is a zingy cake that needs nothing more than a squeeze of lime.

1 baking potato, about ½ pound

1½ pounds fillet of cod or other mild, delicate white fish

1 tablespoon peeled and minced fresh ginger

½ cup minced cilantro leaves, plus more for garnish

1 fresh or dried hot red chile, minced, or ¼ teaspoon cayenne pepper, or to taste

Salt and freshly ground black pepper

2 teaspoons peanut or vegetable oil

Lime wedges

1 Boil the potato in salted water to cover until it is tender but not mushy, 30 to 40 minutes.

2 Meanwhile, place the fish in a skillet that can later be covered. Add water to cover, salt the water, and bring to a boil over high heat. Cover, turn off the heat, and set a timer for 10 minutes. Use a slotted spoon to remove the fish to a bowl.

3 When the potato is done, peel it and mash it with the fish. Add the ginger, cilantro, and chile, along with some salt and pepper to taste, and work the mixture with your hands until it is well blended. Shape into 8 equal burger-shaped patties.

4 Preheat the broiler and set the rack about 4 inches from the heat source. Brush the patties on both sides with the oil, then place on a nonstick baking sheet. Broil carefully until nicely browned on top, then turn and brown on the other side. Sprinkle with more cilantro and serve hot with lime wedges.

WINE Nothing too serious; a crisp white, like Muscadet or Pinot Grigio, a light red, like Chianti, a no-name wine from the south of France, or an inexpensive rosé.

SERVE WITH You definitely need some crisp coolness here, so serve a salad, or coleslaw for that matter.

STARCHY, "BAKING" POTATOES are best here.

FISH CAKE RECIPES USUALLY recommend shaping and refrigerating the cakes for an hour or more. This is not a bad idea—it firms up the cake without changing its delicate nature, allowing it to withstand the rigors of pan-frying—but this step isn't always necessary, because a good fish cake can gain a perfectly crisp, golden crust with the aid of a moderately hot, carefully watched broiler.

OF COURSE, YOU CAN ASSEMBLE these cakes with leftover fish and leftover mashed potatoes, and this is especially easy if you can think far enough ahead to prepare extras of each from preceding meals. (While the three-to-one proportion is ideal, you can make these cakes with one part fish to one part potato if you like.)

WORTH THINKING ABOUT, TOO, is boiling the potatoes and poaching the fish hours or even a day or two in advance; with this out of the way, the cakes can be assembled and broiled in about twenty minutes.

Pan-fried Fish Cakes: Increase the oil to ⅓ cup, or more if necessary. Heat oil in a large skillet (the oil should be at a depth of about 1/16 inch) over medium-high heat. When it is hot (a pinch of the fish mixture will sizzle immediately), add the cakes. Cook, turning once, until brown on both sides, about 10 minutes total.

■ Substitute minced garlic, shallot, scallion, or onion for the ginger, and parsley or other herb(s) for the cilantro.

■ Season with a grating of nutmeg or a teaspoon or more of curry powder (in place of the seasonings in the original recipe).

■ Add ¼ cup or more sour cream and a little butter to the potato as you mash it.

■ Add minced yellow or red bell pepper to the mix.

■ Serve with Mayonnaise (page 192), Worcestershire sauce, tartar sauce, or any other condiment.

Flounder Poached in Broth

Thin fish fillets can be tricky to prepare, mostly because they fall apart the instant they're overcooked. But the fact that quarter-inch-thick fillets of flounder, sole, and other flatfish take so little time to cook can be an advantage. By poaching them in barely hot liquid, you slow the cooking and gain control. By flavoring the liquid first with a quick-cooking aromatic vegetable, you create a dish that only needs bread or rice to become a meal. Unlike with broiling or sautéing, the fish never dries out.

2 cups chicken stock (or one 14- or 15-ounce can)
Three 1-inch-thick leeks
1½ pounds flounder or other thin fish fillets
Salt and freshly ground black pepper

1 Place the stock in a large skillet that can be covered and turn the heat to high. Let it boil and reduce by about half while you prepare the leeks. Trim the leeks of the root and green end; cut the white part in half the long way and rinse thoroughly. Chop each half into ⅛- to ¼-inch-thick semicircles, adding them to the boiling broth as you cut them.

2 When all the leeks are added, cook for another minute. Add salt and pepper to taste and stir, then add the fish. Cover and turn off the heat, or keep the heat at an absolute minimum. Uncover and check the fish after 3 minutes; it is done when a thin-bladed knife encounters no resistance. Continue to check every minute until the fish is done.

3 Serve the fish with the leeks and some broth spooned over it; top all with a sprinkling of coarse salt.

WINE An off-dry white, like Gewürztraminer or Riesling, or a dry Riesling or Pinot Blanc.

SERVE WITH This is a light main course, and to make it a meal you would probably want to precede it with a heavier dish, like pasta—Pasta with Red Wine Sauce, page 38, for example—then serve a salad afterward.

THE TRADITIONAL LIQUID FOR POACHING fish is court bouillon, a stock made from scratch using fish bones, onions, carrots, and celery enhanced with white wine and herbs. Assuming you don't have any court bouillon on hand—and who does?—my poaching liquid of choice is chicken stock, and the canned variety is fine, because you're going to add flavor to it, and quickly, in the form of leeks and fish.

THIS RECIPE TAKES JUST FIFTEEN minutes from start to finish. While the stock comes to a boil and reduces slightly in volume, clean and chop some leeks, adding them to the liquid as they're ready. A couple of minutes later, season the broth and add the fillets. The subsequent cooking time depends largely on your equipment. If you have an electric stove, simply turn the heat off; the element will remain warm enough to cook the fish. You may need a low flame with a gas stove, but it should be the minimum. A heavy-duty pan may retain enough heat to make even that unnecessary.

- Use any aromatic vegetable you like in place of the leeks, alone or in combination: shallots, onions, scallions, garlic, celery, or carrots (cut carrots into very small pieces, or shred them on a grater or in a food processor so they'll cook quickly).

- Add herbs, especially parsley, chervil, or dill, alone or in combination.

- Add spices, alone or in combination. For example, for a North African–style dish, use a few coriander seeds, a small piece of cinnamon, and a little cumin. Or add a couple of teaspoons of curry powder to the broth.

- You can also use this technique for thicker fillets, like red snapper, sea bass, or cod. After you cover the skillet, keep the heat on low and, after about six minutes, check the fish every minute. When a thin-bladed knife encounters no resistance, the fish is done; when it begins to flake, it's overdone—but only slightly, and it will still be juicy.

Sparkling Cider–Poached Fish

TIME: 15 minutes
MAKES: 4 servings

This is a simple marriage of butter, shallots, and mushrooms, splashed in a dose of hard cider (the dry, sparkling kind from France or England, sold nearly everywhere you can buy beer and wine), and used to poach fish in a hot oven. The fish can be haddock, cod, monkfish, halibut, red snapper, or any other white-fleshed fish. The cider provides a distinctively sour fruitiness, not at all like white wine, and the completed dish has complementary textures: crunchy shallots, meaty mushrooms (portobellos are good here), and tender fish.

1 tablespoon butter, or more

½ cup sliced or minced shallots

1 cup roughly chopped portobello or other mushrooms

1½ pounds any white-fleshed fillet of fish, such as cod or red snapper, about 1 inch thick, in 1 or 2 pieces

Salt and freshly ground black pepper

1 cup dry sparkling cider

1 Preheat the oven to 500°F. Smear the bottom of an ovenproof skillet with the butter; sprinkle the shallots and mushrooms around the sides of the skillet. Season the fish with salt and pepper to taste and lay it in the center of the skillet. Pour the cider around the fish.

2 Bring to a boil on top of the stove, then transfer to the oven. Bake for about 8 minutes; it's highly unlikely the fish will need more time than this unless it is very thick (or you like it very well done). Baste with the pan juices and serve.

WINE Cider, or a crisp white like Muscadet or Graves.
SERVE WITH Crusty bread and a salad or green vegetable, like Roasted Asparagus with Parmesan, page 166.

THE LONE IMPROVEMENT YOU CAN MAKE to this dish is to add more butter. Although I stopped at four table-spoons—half a stick—I realized that there really was almost no upper limit as far as my taste buds were concerned. But the dish is awfully nice when made on the lean side, too.

- Substitute any aromatic vegetable, or a combination, for the shallots: onion, leek, carrot (cut very small), celery, fennel, scallions.

- Use a mixture of mushrooms, or fresh mushrooms combined with reconstituted dried mushrooms. A little of the strained mushroom-soaking liquid added to the poaching liquid is nice, too.

- You can enhance the apple flavor and enrich the sauce by adding chopped peeled apples to the mix. Even better, although a little more work is involved, is to peel, core, and slice some apples, then sauté them in butter until tender and lightly browned. Spoon a little over each portion of fish.

- A teaspoon of thyme leaves added to the poaching liquid is great; also good are parsley (a small handful of stalks), chervil (a small bunch), or dill (a few stalks). Garnish with chopped fresh leaves of the same herb.

- Some seeds are good in the poaching liquid, too—try caraway, coriander, or fennel.

Grilled Fish the Mediterranean Way

TIME: 30 minutes
MAKES: 4 servings

It doesn't matter much where you go or to whom you talk: When fishermen, chefs, or home cooks are proud of their fish, they don't fuss with it. One extremely simple preparation, common throughout the Mediterranean, is fish grilled on a bed of fennel stalks. The technique, undoubtedly as old as grilling itself, solves a couple of problems at once: It seasons the fish subtly and without effort, and it helps prevent the fish from sticking to the grill and falling apart. In fact, this method allows you to grill even relatively delicate fillets like cod, usually among the most challenging because of their tendency to fall apart as they near doneness.

4 to 6 fennel or dill stalks, each at least 6 inches long

Four 6-ounce halibut fillets, or 1½ pounds any white-fleshed fish fillet, such as striped bass, monkfish, or cod

Salt and cayenne pepper

1 teaspoon fennel or dill seeds

1 lemon

2 teaspoons extra virgin olive oil

1 Preheat a charcoal or gas grill (for broiling instructions, see the variation below); the fire should be quite hot, and the grill rack about 4 inches from the heat source.

2 When the grill is ready, make a bed of the fennel or dill stalks. Sprinkle the fish lightly with salt and cayenne to taste and lay it (skin side down, if there is a skin side) directly onto the fennel or dill. Close the grill if possible and cook, without turning, until the fish is done—it will be just about opaque all the way through, and offer no resistance to a thin-bladed knife—about 10 minutes.

3 While the fish is cooking, mince or grind the fennel or dill seeds. Cut about 1 inch off each end of the lemon and juice those pieces; slice the remaining lemon as thinly as you can.

4 When the fish is done, remove it from the grill, leaving as much of the stalks behind as possible (some of the burned fronds will adhere to the fish; this is fine). Sprinkle the fish with the fennel or dill seeds, then decorate it with the lemon slices. Drizzle with the lemon juice and olive oil and serve.

WINE Provençal or another inexpensive rosé is ideal.

SERVE WITH You might start with Clam Chowder, page 14, or serve the fish with Grilled Bread Salad, page 24.

THIS IS ONE OF THOSE RECIPES in which the shopping may take you longer than the cooking, because fennel stalks—or those from dill, which are nearly as good—are almost always discarded by grocers. When you buy a bulb of fennel, you're buying the bottom, trimmed of its long stalks; when you buy a bunch of dill, you're buying the feathery tops, trimmed of the stalks that support them. Because this recipe requires some of those stalks, you will probably have to speak directly to a produce manager, visit a farm stand or a friend's garden, or simply get lucky.

IT'S WORTH SPENDING THE FEW minutes it takes to convert a single halibut steak into fillets. A good fishmonger will do this for you, but it's easy: Just use a sharp, thin-bladed knife and cut straight down, following the outline of the bone; each halibut steak will produce four fillets. If you buy a one-and-a-half-inch-thick piece of fish, each fillet will be the perfect serving size. Alternatively, use striped bass (preferably skin-on and scaled), monkfish, cod (also best with the skin on), or any other fillet with some substance. Do not attempt to grill flatfish such as flounder or sole.

Broiled Fish on Fennel or Dill: Preheat the broiler and place the rack as close to the heat source as possible. Put about ½ inch of water in the bottom of a roasting pan and lay the fennel or dill stalks in it. Sprinkle the fish lightly with salt and cayenne pepper and lay it (skin side down, if there is a skin side) directly onto the fennel or dill. Broil until the fish is lightly browned on top and opaque throughout, about 10 minutes. (If at any time the fish is browning too quickly, move the broiler rack down a notch.) Finish as above.

Grilled or Broiled Fish on Fennel or Dill with Butter Sauce: You can take this dish to another level by making a simple butter sauce to serve with it: In a small saucepan, cook 2 tablespoons minced shallot with ⅓ cup each white wine and white wine vinegar, along with a little salt and pepper, until the liquid is almost evaporated. Over the lowest possible heat, stir in ½ to 1 stick of butter, a bit at a time, adding the next bit only when each has been absorbed, until the sauce is smooth and creamy. Serve immediately.

Striped Bass with Mushrooms

TIME: 30 minutes

MAKES: 4 servings

Most fish is so moist that it is difficult to brown it: the surface of the flesh must dry out before it browns and, because fish cooks so quickly, the interior is usually done long before this happens. That's why fish is often coated before cooking; the coating browns much more rapidly than the fish itself.

If, however, you brown only one side of the fillet, that side develops a crisp crust, and the center remains moist. To do this, you preheat your oven to its maximum before beginning to cook (even 600°F is not too hot); start the fish on top of the stove, and immediately move it to the oven, where it will brown beautifully on the bottom, eliminate the need for turning, and remain moist within (as long as it isn't overcooked, of course).

3 tablespoons olive oil

2 tablespoons minced shallot

1 pound mushrooms, preferably a mixture (such as shiitake, crimini, and button), trimmed, rinsed, and sliced

Salt and freshly ground black pepper

1½ to 2 pounds 1-inch-thick fillet of striped bass or other fish, in 1 or 2 pieces, preferably with the skin on

1 teaspoon vinegar

Minced parsley for garnish

1 Preheat the oven to its maximum, at least 500°F; if you have a baking stone, use it. Place 2 tablespoons of the oil in a large skillet and turn the heat to medium. Add the shallots and cook, stirring, until they soften, about 3 minutes. Add the mushrooms and raise the heat to medium-high. Cook, stirring occasionally, until the mushrooms give up their liquid and become tender, about 10 minutes. Season to taste with salt and pepper and keep warm.

2 Meanwhile, heat an ovenproof skillet over high heat. Add the remaining 1 tablespoon oil; when it smokes, add the fish, skin side down. Season the fish with salt and pepper and transfer to the oven; set the timer for 8 minutes.

3 Stir the vinegar into the mushrooms; taste and adjust seasoning. Check the fish when the timer goes off; it is done when the interior is opaque and a thin-bladed knife passes through it with little resistance. Serve the fish, skin (or crisp) side up, on a bed of the mushrooms. Drizzle with the fish pan juices and garnish with the parsley.

WINE This dish is steaklike, and can stand up to a fairly sturdy red, like a good Zinfandel or something from the Rhône region.

SERVE WITH See With Minimal Effort, and consider, too, a good rice or potato dish, or bread and salad.

Keys To SUCCESS

IF YOU HAVE A BAKING STONE, place it in a cold oven before preheating. This technique works equally well with fish with its skin still on and that which has had its skin removed. If the skin is on, it becomes irresistibly crisp and delicious (especially when sprinkled with a little coarse salt). If removed, the flesh becomes crisp, even tough, a nice contrast to the remaining part of the fish, which remains moist and tender.

EVEN WITH THIS TECHNIQUE, a too-thin piece of fish will overcook in the time it takes to brown one side, so don't try this with a fillet of flounder, or even a thin piece of cod. It's best performed with fillets of a near-uniform thickness of about one inch: thicker pieces of cod, for example, center cuts of striped bass or salmon, or a thick piece of sea bass. All of these have edible, delicious skin, so see if you can get a piece that has not had the skin removed—just make sure it has been scaled.

With MINIMAL Effort

Note that this fish cooking technique is independent of the sauce, which means you can omit the mushroom-shallot mixture entirely and serve the fish with a wide variety of accompaniments, including:

- Fig Relish (page 198)
- Cumin-Tomato Relish (page 194)
- Pan-Grilled Tomato Salsa (page 195)
- Parsley-Vinegar Sauce (page 184)
- Red Pepper Puree (page 202)
- Vinaigrette, or any of its variations (pages 186–187)
- Nearly any sauce or salsa you like, or something as simple as a squeeze of lemon, a pat of butter, or a drizzle of good vinegar.

Grilled Tuna with Mesclun Stuffing

TIME: 45 minutes (longer if you have it)
MAKES: 4 servings

One Memorial Day, a friend and I were about to grill a two-inch slab of tuna. The grill was fired up, we made a quick marinade and were washing some greens for a salad. In a flash of inspiration, we decided to combine everything in one dish. We carefully cut a pocket in the tuna—just as if we were stuffing a pork chop—drenched the salad greens in the tuna marinade, and crammed them in there. We closed the pocket with a couple of toothpicks and let the tuna marinate for a while longer. Then we grilled it.

When the tuna was done, we sliced it, exposing lovely rare slices lined with a vein of dressed, barely warm salad. I've made this easy and rather impressive dish several times a year ever since.

Juice of 3 limes
¼ cup high-quality soy sauce
5 tablespoons extra virgin olive oil
2 tablespoons water
1 teaspoon dark sesame oil, optional
½ teaspoon coarsely ground black pepper

2 cups mesclun, arugula, or other greens, washed, dried, and torn into bits
1 tuna steak (about 1½ pounds), no less than 1½ inches thick
Salt and freshly ground black pepper

1 Start a charcoal or wood fire, or preheat a gas grill or broiler. Combine the first 6 ingredients in a bowl or the container of a blender and whisk or blend until emulsified. Soak the greens in this mixture while you prepare the tuna.

2 Make a pocket in the tuna. Be careful not to cut through the top, bottom, or opposite edge of the tuna, and try to keep the entry point relatively small.

3 Drain the greens, reserving the excess marinade, and cram them into the pocket; you can overstuff the tuna (it won't shrink, nor will the greens expand) as long as you don't tear the tuna. If you've kept the pocket opening small, seal it with a toothpick; if it's more than an inch or two wide, use a couple of skewers. Marinate the tuna in the remaining soy mixture until the grill is hot, or up to an hour at room temperature or several hours, refrigerated.

WINE This is not the most wine-friendly dish, but a rough red like Chianti or Zinfandel would not be out of place.

SERVE WITH If you're grilling, a few grilled vegetables and a hunk of bread would go nicely. If you're cooking in the kitchen, a crisp potato dish, or Grilled Bread Salad, page 24.

4 Grill the tuna, turning once, about 6 minutes per inch of thickness (if the steak is 1½ inches thick, for example, turn it after about 4 minutes and cook 4 or 5 minutes more). Cut into ½-inch-thick slices, season with salt and pepper, and serve.

Keys To SUCCESS

WHEN YOU BUY TUNA for this dish, make sure to get a slice that is at least 1½ inches thick; you need a substantial piece for stuffing. As with all tuna, the skin should be removed. Try to find dark-red yellowfin rather than the paler albacore.

With MINIMAL Effort

■ Use this stuffing and marinade with swordfish, salmon, lamb, or beef.

■ Stuff the steaks with pureed roasted garlic; roasted red peppers (or Red Pepper Puree, page 202); about 1 cup chopped fresh herbs; thick pesto; or a mixture of lightly cooked onions, red peppers, and chiles.

■ Substitute any vinaigrette (pages 186–187) for the soy dressing.

Seared Salmon Fillets

TIME: 30 minutes
MAKES: 4 servings

Salmon's flavor is distinctive but chameleonlike, showing itself differently depending on its surroundings. Chef Katy Sparks once demonstrated to me how you can exploit the fickle nature of salmon by varying a few seasonings. One day, Katy and I put some salmon fillets through their paces, flavoring them with rosemary, fennel, and orange; a powder made of porcini and pumpkin seeds; and a variation on the French classic *quatre épices* (four spices). The beauty of Katy's minimalist but infinitely variable system is that the technique remains the same regardless of the herbs or spices used in the coating.

Four 6-ounce skinned salmon fillets

Salt and freshly ground black pepper

1 tablespoon fennel seeds

1 tablespoon minced fresh rosemary

1 tablespoon minced orange zest

2 tablespoons olive oil or butter

1 Season the fillets on both sides with salt and pepper to taste. Grind the fennel seeds coarsely in a coffee or spice grinder, and mix them with the rosemary and orange zest. Press this mixture into the top (nonskin side) of each fillet. Let sit, refrigerated and covered, for up to 24 hours.

2 When you're ready to cook, preheat the oven to 450°F. Preheat a large nonstick skillet over medium-high heat for 3 or 4 minutes. Add the oil or butter and, when it shimmers, place the fillets, coated side down, in the pan. Cook about 1 minute, or until the spice mixture forms a nicely browned crust.

3 Turn the fillets and cook about a minute more, then transfer to the oven. Cook about 4 minutes for rare salmon, 5 to 6 minutes for medium-rare, and 8 minutes for well done.

WINE A good Pinot Noir or a lightly chilled Beaujolais would be great.

SERVE WITH I love any of these fillets on a bed of lightly dressed greens. Another vegetable, some bread, or a crispy potato dish would complete the meal.

WITH UNIFORMLY SIZED FILLETS, the cooking time can be gauged precisely, resulting in the kind of lovely individual pieces of salmon served in restaurants. For four servings, buy one and a half pounds of skinned salmon fillet, taken from the thick (not the tail) end of the fish. Cut across the fillet to make four pieces of equal size.

ALTHOUGH THE TECHNIQUE IS ABOUT as straightforward as can be, allowing the fillets to sit for a while after coating will encourage the fragrant seasonings to permeate the flesh of the fish; try fifteen minutes or so at room temperature, or a couple of hours in the refrigerator.

Seed-Rubbed Salmon: Combine 2 tablespoons raw, shelled pumpkin seeds (pipits) and 2 tablespoons (roughly) dried porcini pieces in a coffee or spice grinder and grind to a coarse powder. Press some of the mixture into the top (nonskin side) of each of the fillets and cook as above.

Spice-Rubbed Salmon: Combine 1 tablespoon coriander seeds or ground coriander, ¼ teaspoon whole or ground cloves, 1½ teaspoons cumin seeds or ground cumin, and 1 teaspoon freshly grated nutmeg (grind all together if necessary). Press some of the mixture into the top (nonskin side) of each of the fillets and cook as above.

■ This technique will work with nearly any spice, herb, or other rub you can think of. Try curry powder; minced lemon zest and parsley; minced lime zest and cilantro; or ground nuts and shallots.

■ Substitute whole or clarified butter, peanut oil, or a neutral oil such as grapeseed or canola for the olive oil.

Salmon Burgers

TIME: 30 minutes
MAKES: 4 servings

There were several reasons I wanted to create a salmon burger. I knew it would taste good, which is reason enough, and I figured it would not necessarily be accompanied by ketchup, another plus. Then there's the fact that salmon is practically ubiquitous and, when on sale, not much more expensive than ground meat.

The challenge, however, was not just to create a salmon burger but a minimalist salmon burger. And here's what I discovered: If you finely grind part of the salmon, it will act as glue for the rest of it, which could be coarsely chopped and therefore retain its moisture during cooking. Coarse bread crumbs keep the mixture from becoming as densely packed as bad meat loaf. And a few simple seasonings help produce a delicious burger in not much more time than it takes to make one from ground round.

1½ pounds skinless, boneless salmon

2 teaspoons Dijon mustard

2 shallots, peeled and cut into chunks

½ cup coarse bread crumbs

1 tablespoon capers, drained

Salt and freshly ground black pepper

2 tablespoons butter or olive oil

Lemon wedges

Tabasco sauce

1 Cut the salmon into large chunks and put about a quarter of it into the container of a food processor, along with the mustard. Turn the machine on and let it run—stopping to scrape down the sides if necessary—until the mixture has become pasty.

2 Add the shallots and the remaining salmon and pulse the machine on and off until the fish is chopped and well combined with the puree. No piece should be larger than ¼ inch or so in diameter, but be careful not to make the mixture too fine.

3 Scrape the mixture into a bowl and, by hand, stir in the bread crumbs, capers, and some salt and pepper. Shape into 4 burgers. (You can cover and refrigerate the burgers for a few hours at this point if you like.)

4 Place the butter or oil in a 12-inch nonstick skillet and turn the heat to medium-high. When the butter foam subsides or the oil is hot, cook the burgers for 2 to 3 minutes per side, turning once. Alternatively, you can

WINE Light red, like Beaujolais, or a Provençal rosé.
SERVE WITH Pretend they're burgers and take it from there.

grill them; let them firm up on the first side, cooking for about 4 minutes, before turning them over and finishing the cooking for just another minute or two. On no account should the burgers be overcooked. Serve the burgers on a bed of greens, or buns, or simply plates, with lemon wedges and Tabasco or any dressing you like.

THE PROCESS IS SIMPLE as long as you have a food processor. A portion of the salmon is finely ground, almost pureed; the machine takes care of that in about thirty seconds. Then the rest of the fish is chopped, by pulsing the machine on and off a few times. The two-step grinding process means that those flavorings that you want finely minced, like garlic or ginger, can go in with the first batch of salmon; those that should be left coarse, like onion or fresh herbs, can go in with the second batch.

THE ONLY OTHER TRICK is to avoid overcooking; this burger, which can be sautéed, broiled, or grilled, is best when the center remains pink (or is it orange?)—two or three minutes per side does the trick.

With MINIMAL Effort

- The mustard, shallots, and capers can be considered optional, so you can combine them or omit them as you like when experimenting.

- Use any fresh herbs, such as parsley, chervil, dill, or cilantro. Add 2 tablespoons or more with the second batch of salmon.

- Use a combination of soy sauce (about a tablespoon), sesame oil (a teaspoon), and ginger (a teaspoon, added with the first batch of salmon). Use peanut oil for sautéing if you have it.

- Add a small clove of garlic along with the first batch of salmon. (Don't overdo it, because the garlic will remain nearly raw and strong-tasting.)

- Add ¼ cup onions or scallions in addition to or instead of the shallots.

- Add spice mixtures such as curry or chili powder to the mixture—a teaspoon to a tablespoon, depending on your preference.

- Add red or yellow bell pepper (about ½ cup), cored, seeded, and roughly chopped, with the second batch of salmon.

- Add ¼ cup or more lightly toasted pignoli nuts or about a tablespoon of sesame seeds along with the bread crumbs.

Gravlax

TIME: About 24 hours, largely unattended
MAKES: At least 12 servings

The intense orange color, meltingly tender texture, and wonderful flavor of gravlax gives it an allure shared by few fish preparations—not bad for a dish whose name means "buried salmon" in Swedish. The curing process intensifies the color, tenderizes the texture, and enhances the flavor. Although most chefs jazz up gravlax with sauces and side dishes, it is brilliant on its own, or with just a few drops of lemon or mild vinegar. And the rankest kitchen novice can make it at home.

1 cup salt

2 cups sugar

1 bunch dill, stems and all, chopped

One 2- to 3-pound fillet of salmon, pin bones removed

1 Mix together the salt, sugar, and dill. Place the salmon, skin side down, on a large sheet of plastic wrap. Cover the flesh side of the salmon with the salt mixture, making sure to coat it completely (there will be lots of salt mix; just pile it on there).

2 Wrap the fish well. If the air temperature is below 70 degrees and it is not too inconvenient, let it rest outside the refrigerator for about 6 hours, then refrigerate for 18 to 24 hours more. Otherwise, refrigerate immediately for about 36 hours.

3 Unwrap the salmon and rinse off the cure. Dry, then slice on the bias. Serve plain, or with lemon wedges, crème fraîche, sour cream, or a light vinaigrette.

WINE Champagne or a good white, preferably Burgundy.
SERVE WITH This is a starter, to be served with bread. Make fresh mustard-scented Mayonnaise (page 192) to serve with it.

SALMON FOR GRAVLAX SHOULD BE as fresh as possible, but this in no way eliminates supermarket fish; most supermarkets receive deliveries of popular fish like salmon three times a week, and farm-raised salmon is often harvested and shipped on the same day. Once you buy it, keep it cold, and keep both your hands and your work surface impeccably clean.

SINCE YOU DON'T EAT THE SKIN of cured salmon, it need not be scaled. But you should check the fillet for pin bones, the long bones that run down the center of the fillet; these are not removed by routine filleting. Press your finger down the center of the flesh and you will feel them; remove them, one at a time, with a needle-nose pliers or similar tool.

THE TIMING FOR GRAVLAX IS IMPRECISE; the longer it sits, the drier and more strong-flavored it will become. So if you're ready for dinner just twenty-four hours after beginning the cure, by all means serve the gravlax; similarly, if you want to hold the cure for an extra twelve or twenty-four hours, feel free. Alternatively, you can rinse off the cure when the gravlax is done and keep it for a couple of days before serving.

YOU MUST TREAT FINISHED GRAVLAX as a fresh product. Keep it well wrapped and refrigerated, and use it within a few days. Freezing is a safe option, but will dry the salmon out to some extent.

Low-Salt Gravlax: Use ½ cup salt and ¼ cup sugar. Combine a couple of chopped bay leaves, ¼ cup shallots, and 1 teaspoon cracked black pepper with the dill. Refrigerate for 48 hours and proceed as above.

Citrus Gravlax: Use 1 cup each salt and sugar, combined with the grated zests of 2 oranges, 2 lemons, 2 limes, and 2 grapefruits; 2 tablespoons juniper berries; 1 tablespoon cracked coriander seeds; and 1 bunch dill, stems and all. Marinate for 12 to 24 hours.

Grilled or Broiled Lobster

TIME: 40 minutes

MAKES: 4 servings

Many people argue that the simplest method of cooking a lobster—boiling it in, or steaming it above salted water—is the best. And if you don't have lobsters often, or you have the perfect lobster, it's hard to counter this argument.

But part of this attitude stems from the fact that the easiest way to kill a lobster is to plop it into a pot of water, cover it, and pray that the lobster isn't strong enough to push the cover off. The alternative, inserting a knife into the lobster's head, does not have universal appeal—to say the least.

But an unwillingness to perform surgery does not mean that you're stuck with plain boiled lobster. There is a way to "par-boil" lobster that will then allow you to grill or broil it without overcooking. The technique, which is outlined here, is easy, foolproof, and perhaps even humane.

Four 1¼- to 1½-pound live lobsters
Salt and freshly ground black pepper

¾ cup Basic Vinaigrette (page 186)

1   Start the charcoal grill if you're using it. Bring a large pot of water to a boil and salt it. Plunge the lobsters into the water (one or two at a time if necessary) and cook just until they turn red, about 2 minutes. Remove the lobsters and plunge them into an ice-water bath to stop the cooking. (You can do this several hours in advance and refrigerate the lobsters until you're ready to proceed.) Split the tails down the middle of their soft sides so they will lie flat.

2   Preheat the broiler if you're using it. With either broiler or grill, adjust the rack so that there will be about 3 inches between the lobsters and the heating source. Broil or grill the lobsters with their flesh side facing the heat until they are hot and their shells just begin to char, about 10 minutes. Sprinkle with salt and pepper and serve hot, warm, at room temperature, or cold, with the vinaigrette.

WINE   Really good white—preferably Chardonnay—though a light red, like Beaujolais or a minor Pinot Noir, would also be good.

SERVE WITH   Grilled vegetables, French fries, and/or a salad.

MAKE SURE YOU BOIL plenty of water for the first step. You want to cook the lobsters barely but quickly. And have an ice-water bath ready to stop the cooking.

■ Serve the lobsters with melted butter or with Mayonnaise, page 192.

■ Make ginger or garlic butter: Melt a stick of butter and add 1 tablespoon minced fresh ginger or garlic; cook gently for about 2 minutes.

■ Roast the lobsters: Step 1 remains the same, but in Step 2, place them, flesh side up, in a 500°F oven. Roast for about 15 minutes. Baste with vinaigrette or with any other sauce while they cook.

■ Use any of the vinaigrette variations on pages 186–187 as a sauce.

Mussels, Asian Style

Most steamed mussel preparations contain parsley, garlic, and white wine, with the occasional addition of tomatoes and herbs. There are, however, other directions in which you can prepare mussels, and they're no more effort than the familiar ones. Generally, there are two easy changes to make: First, use distinctive Asian seasonings such as ginger, soy, or curry powder. And second, omit the cooking liquid. By relying only on the mussels' natural juices, you can add fewer seasonings (and less of each) and still produce a flavorful sauce that is less watery than most.

When you finish mussels with soy, the sauce becomes a lovely shade of mahogany; with curry, it's stunningly yellow. Either way, these are mussel dishes that are better served with rice for sopping up the juices than with bread.

2 tablespoons peanut or canola oil

¼ cup roughly chopped scallions

1 tablespoon roughly chopped fresh ginger

2 cloves garlic, lightly smashed

4 pounds mussels, well washed

1 tablespoon soy sauce

1 Put the oil in a saucepan large enough to hold all the mussels and turn the heat to medium. A minute later, add the scallions, ginger, and garlic and cook, stirring occasionally, for about 1 minute.

2 Add the mussels, turn the heat to high, and cover the pot. Cook, shaking the pot occasionally, until they all (or nearly all) open, about 10 minutes. Turn off the heat.

3 Scoop the mussels into a serving bowl. Add the soy sauce to the liquid, then pass it through a fine strainer (or a coarse one lined with cheesecloth). Pour the liquid over the mussels and serve.

WINE Champagne, beer, or Gewürztraminer.

SERVE WITH If you're serving these as part of a light meal, salad. If you're using them as a starter, follow with a stir-fry (see Ten-Minute Stir-Fried Chicken with Nuts, page 122) and rice.

WHEN CLEANING MUSSELS, DISCARD ANY with broken shells. If the mussels have beards—the hairy vegetative growth that is attached to the shell—trim them off. Those mussels that remain closed after the majority have been steamed open can be pried open with a knife (a butter knife works fine) at the table.

Steamed Mussels with Curry: Substitute butter for the oil. Substitute shallots for the scallions, and omit the ginger and garlic. When the shallots are soft, sprinkle them with 1 teaspoon curry powder and cook, stirring, another 30 seconds. Cook and finish as in main recipe, substituting the juice of 1 lime for the soy sauce.

Steamed Mussels with Fennel: Use olive oil. In place of the scallions and ginger, use 2 or 3 fennel stalks, roughly chopped, and 1 tablespoon fennel or anise seeds; add ¼ cup Pernod or other anise-flavored liqueur if you have it. Omit the soy sauce and finish with a squeeze of lemon.

Thai Steamed Mussels: Use peanut oil. Add 1 lemongrass stalk, roughly chopped; 1 dried hot red chile; and 2 lime leaves to the scallions, ginger, and garlic. Substitute nam pla (fish sauce) for the soy sauce.

Steamed Clams with Soy: Any mussel recipe will work for steamers, which are also known as soft-shell clams. But steamers must be rinsed after shucking to remove all traces of sand, and you don't want to dilute these delicious broths by dipping clams into them one after the other. The solution is to substitute littlenecks—small hard-shell clams, the kind served on the half shell and used for pasta with clam sauce—for the mussels. These contain no sand at all, but because their shells are heavier, use 1½ to 2 pounds of littlenecks to replace each pound of mussels. Proceed exactly as above.

Paella, Fast and Easy

TIME: 30 minutes
MAKES: 4 servings

Although you wouldn't know it from the massive dish served in restaurants, paella has simple roots. The word itself comes not from a fancy combination of rice, seafood, sausage, and meat, but from *paellera*, a large pan that looks like a flat wok. And the only ingredient common to every traditional paella is rice—which makes sense, since the dish originated in Valencia, Spain's great rice-growing region.

Some people argue that a true paella must contain only meat or seafood, never both, that a true paella can be prepared only in a *paellera*, or that true paella must be cooked outdoors over wood. Perhaps they're all right. What's clear to me is that you can produce a fabulous rice dish I call paella in just over half an hour, which makes it a great option for weeknights.

4 cups chicken stock

Pinch saffron, optional

3 tablespoons olive oil

1 medium onion, peeled and minced

2 cups medium-grain rice

Salt and freshly ground black pepper

2 cups raw peeled shrimp, cut into ½-inch chunks

Minced parsley for garnish

1 Preheat the oven to 500°F, or as near that temperature as you can get it. Warm the stock in a saucepan along with the saffron if you're using it. Place an ovenproof 10- or 12-inch skillet over medium-high heat and add the oil. A minute later, add the onion and cook, stirring occasionally, until translucent, about 5 minutes.

2 Add the rice and cook, stirring occasionally, until glossy, just a minute or two. Season liberally with salt and pepper and add the warmed stock, taking care to avoid the rising steam. Stir in the shrimp and transfer the skillet to the oven.

3 Bake about 25 minutes until all the liquid is absorbed and the rice is dry on top. Garnish with parsley and serve immediately.

WINE Albariño, the great Spanish white, would be ideal. A light red wouldn't be bad either.

SERVE WITH You need nothing more than a salad, or a simple vegetable dish. A little bread doesn't hurt. And, if you're feeling ambitious, Piquillo Peppers with Shiitakes and Spinach, page 176.

Keys To SUCCESS

I DON'T HAVE A *PAELLERA*, and I'm not about to buy one, so I use a cast-iron skillet.

THE RICE MUST BE MEDIUM-GRAIN, and since Spanish rice is not easy to find, I generally use Arborio, now sold everywhere.

HALF OF THIS RECIPE WOULD produce an appropriate amount for a side dish for four; use an 8-inch skillet for best results.

With MINIMAL Effort

Shrimp is my first choice for this dish, but the alternatives are numerous; as long as the pieces are less than ½ inch thick, anything will cook through in the time it takes for the liquid to evaporate. And you can combine them at will. Try:

■ Sausage, cut into bits (especially chorizo)

■ Peas and/or other vegetables, cut up if necessary

■ Scallops, treated exactly like the shrimp

■ Boneless pork or chicken, cut into ½-inch cubes or smaller

■ Tofu, stirred into the rice during the last 5 minutes of baking

■ Clams and/or mussels, well scrubbed, placed on top of the rice when you put the pan in the oven

Shrimp with Lemongrass

Shrimp is a perfect weeknight food, not only because it cooks so quickly—usually in less than five minutes—but because it marries well with so many different flavors. One of the best pairings is shrimp and citrus, which includes not only lemon and lime but lemongrass, so named because of its haunting fragrance and subtle but unmistakable flavor.

Lemongrass, once considered exotic, is becoming increasingly easy to find. It is sold in almost every Asian market and even in many supermarkets. Lemongrass is easy to use; it does, however, require what may be an unfamiliar preparation.

2 tablespoons peanut or canola oil

1½ pounds shrimp, peeled

1 tablespoon minced lemongrass

1 teaspoon minced garlic

1 teaspoon minced lime zest or lime leaves

½ cup chicken, fish, or shrimp stock, or water (if necessary)

2 tablespoons nam pla or nuoc mam (fish sauce, available at most supermarkets and all markets selling Southeast Asian ingredients)

Freshly ground black pepper

1 Put the oil in a 10- or 12-inch skillet and turn the heat to medium-high; a minute later, add the shrimp.

2 Cook, undisturbed, until the bottoms of the shrimp turn pink, about 2 minutes. Stir in the lemongrass, garlic, and lime zest or leaves. If the mixture is dry, add the stock or water, then the fish sauce and plenty of black pepper. Serve immediately.

WINE Beer, or a dry Gewürztraminer or Riesling.

SERVE WITH White rice and a salad lightly dressed with a soy vinaigrette (see page 187).

SEE MINTY BROILED SHRIMP SALAD, page 32, for guidance in buying shrimp.

LEMONGRASS DOES NOT REALLY TENDERIZE with cooking, so if the core is on the tough side, you must take care to mince it finely. (Peel off all the exterior layers to reach the relatively tender inner core, which is the part you use.) When minced, each stalk will produce about a tablespoon or even less of usable lemongrass.

■ Made with soy sauce in place of fish sauce, the stir-fry will taste more familiar.

■ Substitute scallops for the shrimp. Cooking time will be just about the same. (Do not overcook the scallops; they should remain translucent in the middle.)

■ Substitute boneless chicken, turkey, or pork, cut into ½-inch to 1-inch chunks, for the shrimp. Cooking time will be somewhat longer; 6 to 8 minutes total.

Shrimp in Yellow Curry

Some Thai dishes are what are usually called curries, containing curry powder and a combination of herbs and aromatic vegetables. A typical dish might feature a mixture of garlic, shallots, chiles, lime leaf, sugar, and galangal or ginger. This curry, which features coconut milk, is just such a dish.

- 2 tablespoons peanut or vegetable oil
- 1 cup minced onion
- 1 tablespoon minced garlic
- 1 tablespoon minced fresh ginger
- 1 teaspoon minced fresh hot chiles, or crushed red pepper flakes, or to taste
- 1 tablespoon curry powder, or to taste
- 1 cup fresh or canned coconut milk
- 1½ to 2 pounds medium-to-large shrimp, peeled
- Salt and freshly ground black pepper
- 2 tablespoons nam pla or nuoc mam (fish sauce, available at most supermarkets and all markets selling Southeast Asian ingredients), or to taste
- ¼ cup chopped cilantro or mint leaves

1 Place the oil in a large, deep skillet and turn the heat to medium. Add the onion, garlic, ginger, and chiles and cook, stirring frequently, until the vegetables are tender and the mixture pasty. Add the curry powder and cook, stirring, another minute.

2 Add the coconut milk and raise the heat to medium-high. Cook, stirring only occasionally, until the mixture is reduced by about half. (If you want to cook the dish a few hours in advance, now is the time to stop. Finishing it will take only 5 or 10 minutes, and is best done just before serving.)

WINE Any bone-dry white will work pretty well; it should be inexpensive, because it will be overwhelmed by the spice. Beer is good, too.

SERVE WITH Definitely rice, with salad or a simple vegetable dish, like Tender Spinach, Crisp Shallots, page 174.

3 Add the shrimp, a few pinches of salt, and a little black pepper and cook, stirring frequently, until the shrimp release their liquid (the mixture will become quite moist again) and turn pink, 5 to 10 minutes. Add 1 tablespoon nam pla, stir, then taste and add the rest if necessary. Garnish with cilantro or mint and serve with white or sticky rice.

Keys To SUCCESS

ALTHOUGH CANNED COCONUT MILK is ridiculously convenient, making coconut milk at home is easy, and contains no preservatives: Combine 2 cups water and 2 cups dried unsweetened shredded or grated coconut in a blender. Use a towel to hold the lid on tightly and turn the switch on and off a few times quickly to get the mixture going. Then blend for about 30 seconds. Let rest for 10 minutes. Pour the milk through a strainer. This will be fairly thick. If you need more milk, just pour additional water through the coconut, up to another cup or two. Press the coconut to extract as much liquid as possible. Use immediately or freeze indefinitely.

With MINIMAL Effort

- Substitute boneless chicken or pork, cut into cubes no bigger than 1 inch across, for the shrimp. Increase cooking time slightly.

- Substitute scallops for the shrimp; cooking time will remain the same.

- Use firm tofu in place of the shrimp; cooking time will remain the same.

- Use skinned, bone-in chicken in place of the shrimp. Cover the skillet, and cook over low heat, stirring every few minutes, until the meat is done. Cooking time will increase significantly, to about 20 to 30 minutes after adding the meat.

Stuffed Scallops

TIME: 30 minutes
MAKES: 4 servings

The sea scallop is one of the most perfect of nature's convenience foods—almost nothing cooks faster. This is especially true if you opt to heat the mollusk until it remains rare in the center, as do most scallop admirers. (Shuckers separate the scallop's meat from its guts soon after capture, which makes scallops the safest shellfish to eat undercooked or even raw.) Sea scallops are also large enough to stuff, not with bread crumbs or other fish, as is common with clams or lobsters, but with herbs, garlic, and other flavorings. As long as a scallop is a good inch across and roughly three-quarters of an inch thick, you can make an equatorial slit in it and fill it with any number of stuffings.

20 large fresh basil leaves

1 small garlic clove, peeled

½ teaspoon coarse salt

¼ teaspoon freshly ground black pepper

3 tablespoons extra virgin olive oil

1¼ to 1½ pounds large sea scallops of fairly uniform size

1 Mince the basil, garlic, salt, and pepper together until very fine, almost a puree (use a small food processor if you like). Mix in a small bowl with 1 tablespoon of the olive oil to produce a thick paste.

2 Cut most but not all of the way through the equator of each scallop, then smear a bit of the basil mixture on the exposed center; close the scallop.

3 Place a large nonstick skillet over high heat for a minute; add the remaining oil, then the scallops, one at a time. As each scallop browns—it should take no longer than 1 or 2 minutes—turn it and brown the other side. Serve hot, drizzled with the pan juices.

WINE A not-too-subtle red, like Chianti, Zinfandel, or something from the south of France.

SERVE WITH Nice following a dish like Spaghetti with Fresh Tomato Sauce (page 50), then served with bread and salad.

ALTHOUGH THESE MAY BE GRILLED or broiled, I sauté them in order to allow the stuffing juices to mingle with those of the mollusks themselves; this liquid makes the scallops perfect to serve over raw or cooked greens.

A WORD ABOUT BUYING SCALLOPS: Many are dipped in a chemical solution to prolong their shelf life. Not coincidentally, this soaking causes them to absorb water, which increases their weight and—water being cheaper than scallops—decreases their value. Furthermore, the added water makes browning more difficult. You can recognize processed scallops by their stark white color; in addition, they are usually swimming in liquid. Buy dry, beige (or slightly pink or orange) scallops from a reliable fishmonger and you won't have a problem.

MANY COOKS REMOVE THE TOUGH little hinge present on one side of most scallops before cooking. But when you're stuffing scallops, leave it on and cut from the side directly opposite. The hinge will then serve the purpose of holding the scallop together, and can be removed at the table or eaten; it's slightly tough, but not unpleasant.

Sautéed Scallops with Herb Paste: You can substitute prepared pesto for the basil mixture above. Alternatively, substitute parsley, cilantro, or dill for the basil in the original recipe.

Stuffed Scallops with Greens: When the scallops are done, place them on a bed of greens (about 6 cups is right for this amount of scallops). Turn the heat under the skillet to low and add 3 tablespoons fresh lemon juice. Cook, stirring, for about 10 seconds, then pour the pan juices over the scallops and greens and serve, drizzled with more olive oil if you like.

Sautéed Scallops Stuffed with Peanut Sauce: Cream 2 tablespoons chunky natural peanut butter with ¼ teaspoon minced garlic, minced fresh chiles or cayenne to taste, 1 teaspoon sugar, and sufficient soy sauce to make a thin paste. Use this paste as you would the basil paste, above, and use peanut oil to sauté the scallops. When the scallops are done, place them on a bed of lightly steamed or sautéed bitter greens, such as dandelions or mustard. Turn the heat under the skillet to low and add 3 tablespoons lime juice. Cook, stirring, for about 10 seconds, then pour the pan juices over the scallops and greens and serve, drizzled with a little more peanut oil if you like.

HONEY-ORANGE ROAST CHICKEN

CHICKEN UNDER A BRICK

CHICKEN WITH RIESLING

CHICKEN WITH RICE

CHICKEN WITH VINEGAR

SPICY CHICKEN WITH LEMONGRASS AND LIME

DEVILED CHICKEN THIGHS

CHICKEN CURRY IN A HURRY

CHICKEN WITH COCONUT AND LIME

CHICKEN WITH SWEET-AND-SOUR SHERRY SAUCE

CHICKEN CUTLETS MEUNIÈRE

TEN-MINUTE STIR-FRIED CHICKEN WITH NUTS

ROAST TURKEY BREAST

TURKEY TONNATO

Poultry

PAN-FRIED DUCK

ROAST DUCK IN ONE HOUR

THE MINIMALIST'S THANKSGIVING TURKEY (FASTEST BREAD
STUFFING, SHERRY REDUCTION SAUCE)

Honey-Orange Roast Chicken

Why has roasting chicken become a daunting task? In fact few dishes are simpler; starting with a good chicken is really the hard part. And roast chicken may be even better if you baste it with flavorful liquid while it's in the oven. Contrary to conventional "wisdom," this does nothing to keep the bird moist—the bird remains moist by itself as long as it isn't overcooked. It does, however, add flavor to the skin and creates a ready-made sauce that can be spooned over the chicken when you serve it.

½ cup orange juice, preferably freshly squeezed

½ cup honey

1 tablespoon ground cumin

Salt and freshly ground black pepper

3-pound chicken, giblets and excess fat removed

1 Preheat the oven to 400°F. To ease cleanup, use a nonstick roasting pan, or line a roasting pan with a double layer of aluminum foil. Combine the orange juice, honey, cumin, salt, and pepper in a blender or a bowl and blend or whisk until smooth. Place the chicken in the roasting pan and spoon all but ¼ cup of the liquid over it, making sure to get some of the liquid on the legs and thighs.

2 Place the chicken in the oven, legs first. Roast 10 minutes, then spoon the accumulated juices from the bottom of the pan back over the chicken. Reverse the pan back to front, and return to the oven. Repeat 4 times, basting every 10 minutes and switching the pan position each time. If the chicken appears to be browning too quickly, lower the heat a bit (see Keys to Success). If the pan dries out (unlikely but possible with an extremely lean bird), use the reserved liquid and, if necessary, some additional orange juice or water.

WINE Red and rich, but not necessarily elegant—something from the south of France, or a Rioja, would be great.

SERVE WITH For some reason, steamed broccoli always does it for me with roast chicken; obviously, any cooked vegetable you like will work fine. Mashed potatoes are great too, as is crusty bread, buttered noodles, rice, or any other simple starch. Starting or finishing with Pear and Gorgonzola Green Salad, page 26, would be magnificent.

3 After 50 minutes of roasting, insert an instant-read thermometer into the bird's thigh; when it reads 155 to 165 degrees, remove the chicken from the oven and baste one final time. Let rest 5 minutes before carving and serving.

Keys To SUCCESS

ADDING HONEY OR SUGAR to the basting liquid helps the bird turn a dark mahogany color. The result is not overly sweet, either, because the caramelized sugars have a bitter, complex component.

THERE IS A CERTAIN BOLDNESS you need to roast a bird this way. After twenty minutes of cooking, you will be certain that the skin is going to burn in spots, but have faith. Rotate the chicken back to front in the oven, continue to baste, and the skin will become uniformly dark brown. If you're convinced that scorching is an issue, lower the heat by 25 to 50 degrees.

REMOVE THE CHICKEN from the oven when an instant-read thermometer inserted into the thickest part of the thigh reads 155 degrees; any traces of pinkness disappear during the few minutes it sits before carving. If this procedure makes you nervous, cook the chicken a little longer, but not beyond 165 degrees.

With MINIMAL Effort

Soy-Roasted Chicken: Replace the orange juice with ¼ cup soy sauce; add 1 teaspoon minced garlic, 1 teaspoon peeled and grated or minced fresh ginger or ½ teaspoon ground ginger, and ¼ cup minced scallions to the liquid; omit the cumin.

Herb-Roasted Chicken: Mix together ¼ cup extra virgin olive oil and 2 tablespoons chopped parsley, chervil, basil, or dill. Baste the chicken with this mixture as it roasts. Garnish with more chopped herbs.

Lemon-Roasted Chicken: Brush the chicken with olive oil before roasting; cut a lemon in half and put it in the chicken's cavity. Roast, more or less undisturbed, until done; squeeze the juice from the cooked lemon over the chicken and carve.

- Substitute paprika for the cumin.

- Add minced garlic to the basting mixture.

- Add some whole cumin seeds to the mixture.

- Add a tablespoon of vinegar or lemon juice to the mixture.

Chicken Under a Brick

TIME: 45 minutes
MAKES: 4 servings

The Italian chicken *al mattone*, or chicken under a brick, is the simplest and best method for producing crisp, delicious skin, and wonderfully moist meat. As a bonus, much of the chicken's own moisture remains at the bottom of the pan; it makes a perfect natural sauce.

1 whole 3-pound chicken, trimmed of excess fat, rinsed, dried, and split, backbone removed

1 tablespoon fresh minced rosemary or 1 teaspoon dried rosemary

Salt and freshly ground black pepper

1 tablespoon coarsely chopped garlic

2 tablespoons extra virgin olive oil

2 sprigs fresh rosemary, if available

1 lemon, cut into quarters

1 Place the chicken on a cutting board, skin side down, and press down as hard as you can with your hands to make it as flat as possible. Mix together the rosemary, salt, garlic, and 1 tablespoon of the olive oil and rub this all over the chicken. Tuck some of the mixture under the skin as well. If time permits, cover and marinate in the refrigerator for up to a day (even 20 minutes of marinating is helpful).

2 When you are ready to cook, preheat the oven to 500°F. Preheat an ovenproof 12-inch skillet (preferably nonstick) over medium-high heat for about 3 minutes. Press the rosemary sprigs into the skin side of the chicken. Put the remaining olive oil in the pan and wait about 30 seconds for it to heat up.

3 Place the chicken in the skillet, skin side down, along with any remaining pieces of rosemary and garlic; weight it with another skillet or one or two bricks or

WINE Red and rough—Chianti is ideal.
SERVE WITH Smooth, creamy mashed potatoes would be nice, as would any other simple starch, including bread; and any vegetable dish you like, such as Fennel Gratin, page 172.

rocks, wrapped in aluminum foil. The basic idea is to flatten the chicken by applying a fair amount of weight evenly over its surface.

4 Cook over medium-high to high heat for 5 minutes, then transfer to the oven. Roast for 15 minutes. Remove from the oven and remove the weights; turn the chicken over (it will now be skin side up) and roast 10 minutes more, or until done (large chickens may take an additional 5 minutes or so). Serve hot or at room temperature, with lemon wedges.

■ Use different herbs in the place of rosemary; sage, savory, tarragon, even paprika, are all great. Or try a light dusting of cinnamon, ginger, and/or other "sweet" spices.

■ Use minced shallots instead of garlic.

■ Vary the acidic ingredient: balsamic, sherry vinegar, or lime juice can all pinch-hit for the lemon, depending upon the other flavors.

■ Use clarified butter or neutral oil such as canola or corn in place of the olive oil.

■ Leave European flavors behind entirely and make the dish Asian, using peanut oil and a mixture of minced garlic, ginger, and scallions. Finish the dish with lime quarters and minced cilantro, or a drizzle of soy sauce and sesame oil.

Keys To SUCCESS

ANY SUPERMARKET BUTCHER WILL SPLIT a chicken for you, or you can do it yourself: Use a knife to cut out the backbone, then press down on the breast to flatten it.

YOU NEED TWO OVENPROOF SKILLETS, or a skillet and a couple of bricks or rocks. At that point weight it with another skillet, clean or foil-wrapped rocks, bricks, or what-have-you. (The weight serves two purposes: It partially covers the chicken, which helps it retain moisture, and it ensures that the flesh of the chicken remains in contact with the skillet, which enables it to brown.)

ONCE COVERED, THE CHICKEN is transferred to a very hot oven to finish cooking. Handling the hot, heavy pan takes two hands—be careful.

Chicken with Riesling

When wine is added to simmering chicken, it's most often dry and white. Yet a quick twist of these rules creates a chicken dish so distinctive that it should be in everyone's repertoire. The key is a slightly sweet white wine whose fruity complexity adds a layer of flavor that no dry white wine ever could.

The roots of Chicken with Riesling lie in the classic Alsatian *poulet au Riesling*, which usually contains cream, bacon, and several other ingredients. This recipe contains no more than loads of sliced onion cooked in a small lump of butter along with the chicken and wine, a quartet that produces a dish of sublime tenderness, creaminess, and depth of flavor.

2 tablespoons butter or neutral oil, such as canola

4 medium-to-large onions (about 1½ pounds), peeled and sliced

Salt and freshly ground black pepper

1½ to 2 cups off-dry Riesling

One 3- to 4-pound chicken, preferably kosher or free-range, cut into 8 or 10 serving pieces

1 Place the butter in a skillet large enough to hold the chicken and turn the heat to medium. Add the onions, a large pinch of salt, and some pepper and cook, stirring occasionally, until the onions soften completely and begin to melt into a soft mass, about 20 minutes.

2 Add 1½ cups of the wine and let it bubble away for a minute, then tuck the chicken pieces among the onions; sprinkle the chicken with salt and pepper. Turn the heat to low and cover the pan.

3 Cook, turning the chicken pieces once or twice, for 40 to 60 minutes, or until the chicken is very tender (the meat on the drumsticks will begin to loosen from the bone). If the dish appears to be drying out at any point, add the remaining wine.

4 Serve the chicken, spooning the onions and their liquid over it.

WINE Dry Riesling works wonders, as does Pinot Blanc.

SERVE WITH Buttered noodles are really great, but white rice or bread is fine. A following salad is lovely.

THE WINE PLAYS SUCH A MAJOR role here that it's worth buying the right one. Finding a good off-dry white is not difficult: Almost any German wine made with Riesling (the grape name will be on the label) will do, except for those labeled *trocken,* which means dry (since dry German wines are unusual, avoiding them is not a major challenge). The best German wines are labeled Qualitätswein mit Prädikat, and any of these with the words *kabinett* or *spätlese* are likely candidates, and any decent wine shop will have a good selection of both of these. Less expensive German wines will work as well also.

ALTHOUGH THE COOKING TIME for Chicken with Riesling is not short, it is largely unattended, and the dish can be made well in advance. In fact, as with many meat-and-liquid preparations, this may be more delicious on the second day. And this is a preparation that you can take in many directions, as you'll see in With Minimal Effort.

- Cook the onions an additional 10 minutes or so before adding the wine until they darken in color and become even softer.

- While the onions are cooking, brown the chicken by placing it, skin side up, in a 500°F oven for about 20 minutes. When you add the chicken to the onions, include some of its juice.

- Tuck a couple of bay leaves and/or a few sprigs of thyme in among the onions after they've begun to soften.

- Sauté about ¼ pound of bacon or salt pork cut into ½-inch chunks in the pan before adding the onions.

- Cook about ½ pound of sliced mushrooms (or an ounce or two of dried porcini mushrooms, reconstituted) along with the onions.

- Cook 1 tablespoon or more of chopped garlic with the onions.

- After cooking, puree the onions and their liquid in a blender for a creamlike sauce; use it to top the chicken.

Chicken with Rice

Chicken with rice is a dish that takes well to shortcuts. For fast weeknight meals, I strip it to its bare essentials: oil, onion, chicken, and rice. Stock makes the best cooking liquid, but water works almost as well, because as it simmers with the chicken they combine to produce a flavorful broth, which is in turn absorbed by the rice.

3 tablespoons olive oil

2 medium onions (about 8 ounces), peeled and sliced

Salt and freshly ground black pepper

1 chicken, cut into serving pieces

1½ cups white rice

Pinch saffron, optional

Freshly minced parsley or cilantro for garnish

Lemon or lime wedges

1 Set 3 cups water to boil in a kettle or covered saucepan. Place the olive oil in a large skillet that can later be covered and turn the heat to medium-high. Add the onions and a sprinkling of salt and pepper to taste. Cook, stirring occasionally, until the onions soften and become translucent, 5 to 10 minutes. Meanwhile, remove the skin from the chicken.

2 Add the rice to the onions and stir until each grain of rice glistens; sprinkle with the saffron and stir again. Nestle the chicken pieces in the rice, add a little more salt and pepper, and pour in the boiling water. Turn the heat to medium-low and cover.

3 Cook for 20 minutes or until all the water is absorbed and the chicken is cooked through. (You can keep this warm over a very low flame for another 15 minutes, and it will retain its heat for 15 minutes beyond that, and still be good warm rather than hot.) Garnish with parsley and serve with lemon or lime wedges.

WINE Any simple, inexpensive red, preferably something rough.

SERVE WITH You don't need much to complete this meal—just a salad or any cooked vegetable. Roasted Asparagus with Parmesan (page 166) would be fabulous.

TO MAKE THE DISH as quickly as possible, begin by boiling water and sautéing the onion at the same time; that way, when it's time to add the rice and the chicken to the skillet, the water is ready to go and the dish takes just another twenty minutes to complete.

TO REDUCE GREASINESS, remove the skin from the chicken before cooking it; in a moist dish such as this, the skin is not especially appetizing anyway.

TO ADD THE YELLOW COLOR that traditionally comes from saffron, many restaurants use turmeric or annatto oil, a dark red oil made by gently heating achiote seeds. Although either of these is acceptable, nothing adds the same exotic flavor and depth of color as a tiny pinch of saffron, so try to stick with that. (When buying saffron, steer clear of the tiny vials that contain a few threads; go to a reputable specialty store or mail-order house and buy either a gram, which will cost you under ten dollars and contain about five hundred threads, or a quarter of an ounce, which will cost about forty dollars and last several years.)

- Use any stock instead of water for richer flavor.

- Substitute pearled barley for the rice.

- If you would like crisp-skinned chicken, sauté or roast it separately and combine it with the rice at the last minute.

- Add sausage or shellfish such as shrimp along with the chicken.

- Add strips of red bell pepper, or pitted olives, capers, chopped tomatoes, and/or shelled peas to the skillet along with the onions.

Chicken with Vinegar

This is just one of several great poultry dishes from the area around Lyon, a region whose famous *poulet de Bresse* is considered by many to be the best chicken in the world. Chef Paul Bocuse learned to make *poulet au vinaigre* as a youth and, some years later, showed considerable audacity by putting what is essentially a peasant dish on the menu of his Michelin three-star restaurant just outside of Lyon. He insisted that it was neither how much work nor the cost of ingredients that determined the worthiness of a dish, but how it tasted. Bravo.

2 tablespoons olive oil

One 3-pound chicken, cut up for sautéing

Salt and freshly ground black pepper

¼ cup minced shallots or scallions

1 cup good red wine vinegar

1 tablespoon butter, optional

1 Preheat the oven to 450°F. Set a large skillet—preferably with steep sides to minimize spattering—over medium-high heat. Add the oil and wait a minute. When it is good and hot, place the chicken in the skillet, skin side down. Cook undisturbed for about 5 minutes, or until the chicken is nicely browned. Turn and cook 3 minutes on the other side. Season with salt and pepper to taste.

2 Place the chicken in the oven. Cook 15 to 20 minutes, or until it is just about done (the juices will run clear, and there will be just the barest trace of pink near the bone). Remove the chicken to an ovenproof platter and place the platter in the oven; turn off the oven and leave the door slightly ajar.

3 Pour most but not all of the cooking juices out of the skillet. Place the skillet over medium-high heat and add the shallots or scallions; sprinkle them with a little salt and pepper and cook, stirring, until they are tender, about 2 minutes. Add the vinegar and raise the heat to high. Cook for a minute or two, or until the powerful smell has subsided somewhat. Add ½ cup water and cook

WINE Not easy, because the dish is so acidic, so choose an inexpensive red and don't worry about it much.

SERVE WITH Mild, creamy mashed potatoes or a rich rice dish would be sensational, along with a sweetish vegetable, like glazed carrots or Beet Roesti with Rosemary (page 170).

for another 2 minutes, stirring, until the mixture is slightly reduced and somewhat thickened. Stir in the optional butter.

4 Return the chicken and any accumulated juices to the skillet and turn the chicken in the sauce. Serve immediately.

THE VARIATIONS ARE NUMEROUS but don't matter all that much; the strong—almost piercing—and singular flavor of vinegar is so dominant that it matters little whether you use shallots or garlic, thyme or tarragon, or little seasoning at all.

MOST WINE VINEGAR SOLD in the United States, even the high-quality brands, have an acidity level of 7 percent; many French vinegars are just 5 percent acidity. So when using strong vinegar, it's best to cut it with some water, as I do here.

Paul Bocuse's *Poulet au Vinaigre:* In Step 1, brown the chicken in 7 tablespoons butter. In Step 3, add 3 tablespoons butter to the reduced vinegar sauce.

■ Substitute chopped garlic or onion for the shallots.

■ Add an herb to the chicken as it's browning: a sprig of tarragon (or a big pinch of dried tarragon), a few thyme sprigs (or a teaspoon of dried thyme), or 5 or 6 bay leaves.

■ Use Champagne, rice, or white wine vinegar.

■ Add about 2 tablespoons of capers to the vinegar as it reduces.

■ Stir a tablespoon or more of Dijon mustard into the sauce just before serving.

Spicy Chicken with Lemongrass and Lime

It may seem absurd, even insulting, to attempt to reduce an entire cuisine to a few flavors, but with just a handful of Thai ingredients—nearly all of which are available in most supermarkets—you can duplicate or even improve upon many of the dishes found in your typical neighborhood Thai restaurant. There are a few ingredients that will be unfamiliar to most American cooks, but there are no complicated techniques involved in either preparing or cooking. This chicken dish, which can be taken in many directions, is a good example.

2 tablespoons peanut or vegetable oil

½ cup minced shallots

1 tablespoon minced garlic

1 tablespoon minced galangal or ginger

1 teaspoon minced fresh hot chiles or crushed red pepper flakes, or to taste

1 teaspoon turmeric

1 teaspoon ground dried cilantro

1 teaspoon sugar

2 lemongrass stalks

One 3-pound chicken, cut into serving pieces

Salt and freshly ground black pepper

1 tablespoon minced lime leaves or lime zest

2 tablespoons nam pla (fish sauce)

¼ cup minced fresh cilantro leaves

1 Place the oil in a large, deep skillet and turn the heat to medium. Add the shallots, garlic, galangal or ginger, and chiles and cook, stirring frequently, until the vegetables are tender and the mixture pasty. Add the turmeric, cilantro, and sugar and cook, stirring, for another minute. Trim the lemongrass stalks of their toughest outer layers, then bruise them with the back of a knife; cut them into sections and add them to the mixture along with 1 cup water.

2 Add the chicken and turn it once or twice in the sauce, then nestle it in the sauce; season with a little salt and pepper to taste. Turn the heat to low and cover the skillet. Cook, turning once or twice, until the chicken is cooked through, 20 to 30 minutes. (You can prepare the

WINE Beer is best.

SERVE WITH Jasmine or other short-grained rice, and a salad; for a big meal, you might make Minty Broiled Shrimp Salad, page 32.

recipe in advance up to this point; cover and refrigerate for up to a day, and reheat before proceeding.)

3 Uncover the skillet and raise the heat to medium-high; turn the chicken skin side down. Let most (but not all) of the liquid evaporate and brown the chicken just a little on the bottom. Stir in the lime leaves or zest and nam pla; taste and adjust seasoning as necessary, then garnish and serve with white rice.

THE BEST FRESH CHILES for Thai cooking are the tiny "bird" (also called Thai) chiles; you can substitute others, or used crushed red pepper.

LEMONGRASS IS SOLD IN MANY SUPERMARKETS these days; make an effort to find some for this dish, for it will not be the same without it.

FOR NAM PLA (FISH SAUCE), you can substitute soy sauce; the dish will take on a different but still successful character.

This same type of preparation is used with many different foods in both Thailand and Vietnam, and most of them not only adapt perfectly to this recipe but are faster to prepare.

■ Use boneless chicken, cut into chunks. Cook only about 5 minutes after adding the chicken and bringing the liquid back to a boil. Or leave boneless breasts or thighs whole; cooking time will be about 10 minutes for breasts to 15 minutes for thighs.

■ Use whole shrimp or scallops, or a combination. Cooking time will be about 5 minutes from the time the liquid returns to a boil.

■ Use chunks of boneless pork or bone-in pork such as lean pork chops. Boneless pork will cook in about 10 minutes (from the time the liquid returns to a boil), bone-in in about 20 minutes.

■ Use chunks of firm tofu, which will cook through in 3 to 5 minutes.

■ Use vegetables in the dish: quartered peeled onions, roughly chopped bell pepper, or chunks of zucchini; add them along with the shallots and other seasonings.

Deviled Chicken Thighs

TIME: 30 minutes
MAKES: 4 servings

Prepared mustard is about as underappreciated as a staple could be. After all, it's all-natural (or pretty much so), completely fat-free, low in calories, and high in flavor. Despite these marked assets, its main role in most households is as a condiment for meat and, perhaps, an occasional ingredient in vinaigrette. In this chicken dish, however—essentially broiled chicken smeared with a spicy mustard paste—it plays a leading role.

8 chicken thighs, or a mixture of thighs and drumsticks

Salt and freshly ground black pepper

⅓ cup Dijon mustard

⅓ cup minced shallots, onions, or scallions

¼ teaspoon cayenne pepper or Tabasco sauce, or to taste

Minced parsley for garnish, optional

1 Preheat the broiler to its maximum, and set the rack about 4 inches from the heat. Season the chicken on both sides and place it in a pan, skin side up. Broil, watching carefully, until the skin is golden brown, about 5 minutes.

2 Meanwhile, combine the mustard, shallots, and cayenne. (If you have a small food processor, just throw them in there and pulse the machine on and off a few times.)

3 When the chicken has browned, remove it from the oven and turn it. Spread just a teaspoon or so of the mustard mixture on the underside of the chicken and broil about 5 minutes. Turn the chicken and spread the remaining mixture on the skin side. Broil until the mustard begins to brown.

4 At this point, the chicken may be done (there will be only the barest trace of pink near the bone, and an instant-read thermometer inserted into the meat will read 160 degrees). If it is not, turn off the broiler and let the chicken remain in the oven for another 5 minutes or so. Garnish with the optional parsley and serve.

WINE Though almost any red wine will do, the slight sweetness of Pinot Noir offsets this dish's mild heat very nicely.

SERVE WITH Bread is good, as are crispy potatoes, along with salad or a cooked vegetable, like Roasted Asparagus with Parmesan, page 166.

IF YOU COAT CHICKEN before cooking, you simply cannot get a crisp skin: Broiling coated chicken almost ensures a quick burn, and baking guarantees sogginess. So broil the chicken, skin side up, until it's crisp. (This has another advantage: You can prepare the coating after beginning to cook the chicken, which cuts down on preparation time.) Then turn it over, flavor the underside, and let that cook for a few minutes. After coating the top, return the chicken to the broiler for a final browning; the result is skin that's crisp but not burned.

YOU CAN MAKE THIS DISH with chicken breasts if you prefer, but I recommend that you start with bone-in breasts and follow the same procedure. If you want to use boneless, skinless breasts (forget about crispness) smear the meat all over with the mustard mixture, then broil for just about six minutes, turning two or three times to prevent burning.

■ For extra crunch, combine the mustard and shallots with about 1 cup bread crumbs. Be especially careful in broiling, for the bread crumbs will burn very soon after they brown.

■ For extra flavor, combine the mustard and shallots with about ½ cup chopped parsley (or basil, cilantro, dill, or chervil). Proceed as above.

■ You can use the same coating with pork or veal chops; they should be at least 1 inch thick, Cooking time will be about the same.

Chicken Curry in a Hurry

TIME: 15 minutes
MAKES: 4 servings

Preblended curry powder is one of the original convenience foods, a venerable spice rub and all-purpose flavor-booster. I like to use it in tandem with a twenty-first-century convenience food, the boneless, skinless chicken breast. Even a breast from a good chicken is about as bland as meat can get, and one from the supermarket is not much more flavorful than unsauced pasta: curry changes that quickly.

1 tablespoon canola, corn, or other neutral oil

1 medium onion, peeled and sliced

Salt and freshly ground black pepper

1½ teaspoons curry powder, or to taste

1 pound boneless, skinless chicken breasts, in 4 pieces

1 cup sour cream

Minced cilantro or parsley leaves for garnish

1 Place the oil in a large skillet and turn the heat to medium-high. A minute later, add the onion. Sprinkle with some salt and pepper and cook, stirring occasionally, until translucent, about 5 minutes. Turn the heat to medium, sprinkle with about half the curry powder, and continue to cook for a minute or two.

2 Meanwhile, season the chicken with salt and pepper to taste and sprinkle it with the remaining curry powder. Move the onion to one side of the skillet and add the chicken in one layer. Cook for about 2 minutes per side; remove to a plate.

3 Add the sour cream and stir constantly over medium-low heat until the mixture is nice and thick. Return the chicken to the skillet and cook for 2 more minutes, turning once. Garnish and serve with plenty of white rice.

WINE Slightly off-dry Riesling or Gewürztraminer, or beer.

SERVE WITH Rice is pretty much essential. A salad, or even simpler, some cut-up-and-salted cucumbers, would be a nice counterpoint.

THIS DISH IS SO FAST that you must begin cooking white rice, the natural accompaniment, before even chopping the onion.

SELECT A GOOD CURRY POWDER (supermarket varieties are acceptable but not exciting). If you like shopping by mail, you might choose from among the mixtures offered by Penzey's, a reliable Wisconsin-based spice house (800-741-7787); their vindaloo powder is sweet and not too hot. In the supermarket, look for the Sun brand of Madras curry powder.

YOU'LL HAVE TO CHOOSE between yogurt and sour cream, each of which has advantages. Yogurt is lower in fat, and adds more tang to the dish; but it must be handled carefully and never allowed to boil or the sauce will curdle. (See With Minimal Effort.) Sour cream not only can take more abuse during cooking, it produces a sauce that is creamy beyond compare. It's a can't-lose decision, really, and you may want to try both.

Chicken Curry with Yogurt: Because yogurt will curdle if it boils, some extra care must be taken here: In Step 3, turn the heat to very low and wait a minute before adding the yogurt. Stir the yogurt into the onion and cook, stirring constantly and over low heat, until the yogurt is hot. Return the chicken to the skillet and cook for 2 more minutes, turning once. At no point should the sauce boil.

■ Add nuts (slivered almonds are best), raisins, and/or dried coconut pieces to the onion as it cooks.

■ Add a couple of dried hot red chiles, or crushed red pepper flakes to taste, along with the onion; add more at the end of cooking if you like.

■ Substitute peeled shrimp, or thin-sliced beef or pork, for the chicken; in each case, cooking time will be marginally shorter.

Chicken with Coconut and Lime

I had something like this on a visit to Bangkok, chicken with a creamy but spicy lime sauce. At first I thought the rich texture had come from a pan reduction or even a béchamel-like sauce, but I detected the faint taste of coconut and realized it was little more than coconut milk spiked with lime. With canned coconut milk, it can be made in less than a half hour.

2 limes

1 to 1½ pounds boneless, skinless chicken breasts, in 4 pieces

½ cup canned or fresh coconut milk

Salt and ground cayenne pepper

1 teaspoon nam pla (fish sauce), optional

4 minced scallions for garnish

¼ cup minced cilantro for garnish

1 Remove the zests from the limes with a zester or vegetable peeler (if you use a peeler, scrape off the white inside of the zest with a paring knife). Mince the zest and juice the limes. Marinate the chicken in half the lime juice while you preheat the broiler; adjust the rack so that it is about 4 inches from the heat source. (You may grill the chicken if you prefer.)

2 Warm the coconut milk over low heat; season it with salt (hold off on salt if you use the nam pla) and a pinch of cayenne. Add the lime zest.

3 Put the chicken, smooth (skinned) side up, on an ungreased baking sheet lined with aluminum foil and place in the broiler. Add half the remaining lime juice to the coconut milk mixture.

4 When the chicken is nicely browned on top, about 6 minutes later, it is done (make a small cut in the thickest part and peek inside if you want to be sure). Transfer it to a warm platter. Add the nam pla, if you're using it, to

WINE This is not a wine-friendly dish: Drink beer or water.

SERVE WITH A natural with white rice, of course, especially sticky rice. Some sautéed shiitake mushrooms—or any sautéed vegetables—would make a great side dish, as would Quick Scallion Pancakes, page 178.

the coconut milk; taste and adjust seasoning as necessary. Spoon a little of the sauce over and around the breasts, then garnish with the scallions and cilantro and sprinkle with the remaining lime juice. Serve with white rice, passing the remaining sauce.

Keys To SUCCESS

COCONUT MILK ISN'T THE WATERY liquid from the inside of a coconut, but a thick cream obtained by pressing hot water through grated coconut meat. It's sold in cans in every Asian food store and many supermarkets in the United States, at about a dollar for thirteen ounces. But coconut milk is easy to make yourself, and because you only need a small quantity for this recipe it may make sense to do so (see page 95 for details).

IN THAILAND, THE SAUCE WAS flavored with fresh lime leaves; since these are difficult to find here, I use lime zest, which is a decent substitute.

YOU MIGHT GRILL THIS CHICKEN, but unless you had the grill going for other reasons, I wouldn't bother; it won't add significant flavor during the short cooking time and, besides, the sauce is the real star here. Broiling the boneless breasts without turning allows them to brown nicely on top while they cook without toughening.

With MINIMAL Effort

This same sauce can be used with many different foods:

- Grilled or broiled shrimp or scallops, with the cooking time reduced by a minute or two.

- Boneless pork cutlets, treated like the chicken, with the cooking time increased by a couple of minutes (turn it once during cooking).

- Almost any white-fleshed fillet of fish, especially firmer ones such as grouper, red snapper, or monkfish.

You can also make changes to the sauce:

- Add a pinch or more of cayenne, or a teaspoon of curry powder.

- Add a tablespoon of minced shallot to the coconut milk as it warms.

Chicken with Sweet-and-Sour Sherry Sauce

TIME: 20 minutes
MAKES: 4 servings

Chicken breasts are so bland that they demand something—a spice rub, a salsa, or a strong reduction sauce. Reduction sauces (see page 188) can be made by splashing some water into a skillet after you've roasted or sautéed meat or vegetables in it. The water gathers up the remaining bits, all of which have been nicely browned, and absorbs their flavor. As the quantity of water reduces, the flavor becomes more concentrated and the water is transformed into a sauce.

But if you start with strong-tasting solids and add a variety of bold liquids, reducing each one to a syrupy consistency, you end up with an intense and complex reduction sauce. The process can involve esoteric ingredients and procedures, or it can be quite straightforward, like this one, which is direct, quick, and easy, especially considering that the result is a dark, complex sauce that can be used in many ways.

1 tablespoon plus 1 teaspoon olive oil

½ cup oyster or shiitake mushrooms, trimmed and roughly chopped (discard the shiitake stems or reserve them for stock)

¼ cup sliced shallots

2 teaspoons honey

2 tablespoons sherry vinegar or good-quality wine vinegar

⅓ cup dry sherry (do not use "cream" sherry)

1 cup meat, chicken, or vegetable stock

4 pieces boneless, skinless chicken breasts, 1 to 1½ pounds

Salt and freshly ground black pepper

1 Preheat the broiler or grill. Place a 10-inch skillet over medium-high heat for a minute or two. Add the tablespoon of olive oil, then the mushrooms and shallots, and turn the heat to high. Cook, stirring occasionally, until the mushrooms brown nicely on the edges, about 5 minutes.

2 Add the honey and stir until it evaporates, less than a minute. Add the vinegar and cook, stirring occasionally, until the mixture is dry, about 2 minutes. Add the sherry and cook, stirring once or twice, until the mixture is syrupy and nearly dry, about 5 minutes. Add the stock and cook, stirring once or twice, until the mixture thickens slightly, about 5 minutes. Reduce the heat to medium-low and keep warm.

WINE Dry sherry is fun to drink with meals (remember, however, that it is "fortified," and therefore higher in alcohol than other wines); a soft red like Rioja will also complement this well.

SERVE WITH Crispy bread will sop up this sauce beautifully, but rice or simple buttered noodles are also nice. A bright green vegetable, like broccoli or Green Beans with Lemon, page 168, looks great here; a salad will also go well.

3 Sprinkle the chicken breasts with salt and pepper and grill or broil them for about 6 minutes, or until cooked through.

4 When the chicken is done, season the sauce to taste with salt and pepper and strain it if you like; stir in the remaining olive oil. Serve the chicken with the sauce spooned over it.

Mushrooms and Shallots with Sweet-and-Sour Sherry Sauce: Sauté about 1 pound fresh mushrooms, sliced (a combination of different mushrooms is best, but you can use all shiitakes or all button if you like) in 2 tablespoons olive oil over medium-high heat. The mushrooms will first give up their liquid, then begin to brown. When they start to crisp up, add ¼ cup minced shallots. Cook another 3 or 4 minutes, then serve with the sauce.

■ Sauté the chicken breasts, using the recipe for Chicken Cutlets Meunière (page 120), and serve with the sauce.

■ Serve the sauce with poached, grilled, or sautéed shrimp.

Keys To SUCCESS

USE DRY, OR JUST OFF-DRY, sherry for this sauce, not cream sherry. "Fino," the driest sherry, is widely available; you can also use Oloroso, Amontillado, or Manzanilla, all sold in most liquor stores.

FOR ADDED ELEGANCE, YOU CAN strain the sauce before serving it. Because the mushroom-and-shallot mixture that forms the solid base of the sauce does not give up all of its flavor during this brief cooking—in fact, the mushrooms are chewy and sweet when the sauce is done—I like to spoon the sauce over the chicken without straining.

THIS SAUCE MAY BE PREPARED well in advance. You can keep it warm over low heat for up to an hour, stirring it occasionally, or refrigerate it for a day or two, reheating it (thin with stock or water if necessary) just before adding the teaspoon of olive oil and serving.

Chicken Cutlets Meunière

TIME: 20 minutes

MAKES: 4 servings

"Meunière" once referred to fillets of sole that were floured and quickly sautéed in clarified butter, then finished with parsley, lemon juice, and a little melted butter. Over the years its definition has expanded, to the point where it describes a series of flexible techniques that can be applied to just about any thin cut of meat, poultry, or fish, all of which makes it more useful. The procedure is great with boneless, skinless chicken breasts, and once you have it perfected (it won't take much practice, I promise), you'll be able to apply it to so many foods that months will pass before you repeat yourself. Vary the seasonings in some of the ways described below and the possibilities become even greater, and that's without finishing the dish with a pan-reduction sauce (see page 188).

4 boneless, skinless chicken cutlets (2 breasts), 1 to 1½ pounds

Salt and freshly ground black pepper

Flour or cornmeal for dredging

Olive or other oil (or clarified butter) as needed

1 tablespoon fresh lemon Juice

2 tablespoons minced parsley leaves

1 to 2 tablespoons butter, optional

1 Heat a 12-inch skillet, preferably nonstick, over medium-high heat for about 2 minutes. While it is heating, sprinkle the chicken breasts with salt and pepper to taste and place the flour or cornmeal on a plate.

2 Place the oil or clarified butter in the skillet—it should coat the bottom well—and turn the heat to high. When the oil is hot, dredge a piece of the chicken in the coating, turning it over a few times and pressing it down so that it is well covered. Add the piece to the pan, then repeat with the rest of the chicken.

3 Cook until the chicken is nicely brown on the first side, 3 to 5 minutes, then turn. Cook on the second side 2 to 4 minutes—lower the heat a bit if the coating begins to scorch—until the chicken is firm to the touch. As the chicken is cooking, melt the optional butter over medium heat until it is nut-brown.

4 When the chicken is done, drain it briefly on a paper towel, then transfer to a warm platter. Drizzle with

WINE Can be served with a good, rich white—Chardonnay is best—or a decent-to-fine red, from Beaujolais to Bordeaux.

SERVE WITH Almost any potato dish, especially mashed potatoes or a gratin; a crisp salad; almost any vegetable, especially Tender Spinach, Crisp Shallots, page 174.

lemon juice and top with half the parsley. At the last minute, pour the browned butter over all, add the remaining parsley, and serve.

Keys To SUCCESS

YOU MUST USE A LARGE, flat-bottomed skillet, preferably nonstick, with deep, sloping sides, which makes turning the cutlets easier and keeps the inevitable spattering to a minimum.

PREHEAT THE SKILLET BEFORE YOU add the oil, and make sure the fat is hot before you add the meat; a chopstick or a pinch of flour will sizzle when dipped or tossed into the oil.

MAKE SURE TO USE ENOUGH OIL (or clarified butter, if you're feeling extravagant) to cover the bottom of the skillet; meat that does not come in contact with the oil will essentially steam and turn soggy rather than sauté and become crisp. Do not crowd the food as it cooks; it's far preferable to work in batches (finished pieces keep well in a 200°F oven) than to cram pieces on top of one another.

THE LITTLE BIT OF BROWNED BUTTER added at the end is obviously a luxury, but hearing and seeing the lemon juice and parsley sizzle when the butter hits them—preferably at the table, so everyone can enjoy it—is a thrill.

With MINIMAL Effort

■ For the chicken, you can substitute similarly shaped cutlets of pork, turkey, or veal, all of which will cook through in 6 to 8 minutes, just like the chicken. Shrimp, scallops, and calf's liver can also be cooked this way, all for somewhat less time—generally 4 to 6 minutes.

■ Chicken breasts made this way can be prepared in advance and served at room temperature; don't hold them for more than a couple of hours, however.

■ Substitute bread crumbs (season them with finely minced garlic and parsley if you like), ground nuts, or sesame seeds for the flour or cornmeal.

■ Stir a tablespoon or more of any spice mixture, such as chili powder or curry powder, into the coating.

■ Add a clove of garlic and/or a small handful of chopped herbs to the browning butter.

■ Add a teaspoon of balsamic vinegar and/or a tablespoon of capers to the browning butter (omit the lemon juice).

Ten-Minute Stir-Fried Chicken with Nuts

TIME: 15 minutes

MAKES: 4 servings

Stir-frying—the fastest cooking method there is—can change your life. You can use it for almost anything, and it can be so fast that the first thing you need to do is start a batch of white rice. In the fifteen or twenty minutes it takes for that to cook, you can not only prepare the stir-fry but set the table and have a drink.

1 tablespoon peanut or vegetable oil

2 cups red bell pepper strips, onion slices, or a combination of the two

1 pound boneless skinless chicken breasts, cut into ½- to ¾-inch-thick chunks

1 cup halved walnuts, whole cashews, or other nuts

3 tablespoons hoisin sauce

1   Place the oil in a large, nonstick skillet (12 inches is best) and turn the heat to high; a minute later, add the vegetable(s) in a single layer and cook, undisturbed, until they begin to char a little on the bottom, about 1 minute. Stir and cook 1 minute more.

2   Add the chicken and stir once or twice. Again, cook until the bottom begins to blacken a bit, about a minute. Stir and cook another minute; by this time the vegetables will have softened and the chicken will be done, or nearly so (cut into a piece to check). Lower the heat to medium.

3   Stir in the nuts and the hoisin sauce. Cook for about 15 seconds, then add 2 tablespoons water. Cook, stirring, until the sauce is bubbly and glazes all the chicken and vegetables. Serve immediately, with white rice.

WINE   Stir-fries are not super-wine-friendly, but Champagne is always great, and just slightly off-dry Riesling or Gewürztraminer work well. Beer is another good option.

SERVE WITH   All you really need is rice, but stir-fried noodles, a crisp pan-fried noodle cake, or Quick Scallion Pancakes (page 178) are even better.

A FLAT-BOTTOMED SKILLET—THE LARGER the better, and preferably nonstick—is better than a wok for stir-fries made at home. Keep the heat high and don't stir too much to ensure nicely browned, even slightly charred meat and vegetables.

KEEP IT SIMPLE; TOO MANY INGREDIENTS slow you down, and eventually overload the skillet so that browning becomes impossible.

LOOK FOR A BRAND OF HOISIN sauce whose first ingredient is fermented soybeans rather than sugar or water; the flavor will be more intense.

FOR MANY STIR-FRIES MADE at home, it's necessary to parboil—essentially precook—"hard" vegetables like broccoli or asparagus. So in this fastest-possible stir-fry, I use red bell peppers, onions, or both; they need no parboiling and become tender and sweet in three or four minutes. If you cut the meat in small cubes or thin slices, the cooking time is even less. I include nuts for three reasons: I love their flavor, their chunkiness adds great texture (I don't chop them at all), and the preparation time is zero.

■ Substitute any vegetable, or combination, for the onions and peppers. Try cut-up and par-boiled (simmered in boiling water just until slightly tender) broccoli, asparagus, green beans, or dark leafy greens; shredded raw cabbage; raw snow peas; or chopped tomatoes.

■ Use any boneless meat in place of the chicken, or shrimp or scallops. Cooking time will remain the same.

■ Sprinkle the meat with about 1 tablespoon curry powder as it cooks.

■ Along with the hoisin, add ground bean paste (about 1 tablespoon), plum sauce (about 1 tablespoon), or chili-garlic paste (about ½ tea-spoon, or to taste) during the last minute of cooking.

■ Replace the hoisin with 3 or 4 dried hot red chiles (optional), 1 tablespoon minced garlic, 1 tablespoon soy sauce, and ½ cup chopped scal-lions, all added along with the nuts.

Roast Turkey Breast

TIME: About 1 hour
MAKES: 6 to 10 servings

One 3- to 6-pound turkey
breast

2 tablespoons olive oil, melted
butter, or chicken stock,
optional

Salt and freshly ground black
pepper

There are plenty of reasons to consider cooking a turkey breast for Thanksgiving instead of an entire bird. It minimizes fuss; cuts roasting time at least in half, and usually more; reduces the hassle of carving; and makes the overabundance of leftover turkey somewhat less absurd. It also de-emphasizes the bird, which frees you to concentrate a little more on side dishes, always the most interesting part of the Thanksgiving meal.

Perhaps the greatest advantage to roasting a turkey breast is that you can produce white meat that is truly moist—as opposed to the dried-out white meat that is the near-inevitable result of roasting a whole turkey until the legs are cooked through. Perfectly cooked white meat (all you need is an instant-read thermometer) does not require tons of gravy to become edible, although you may like to serve it with a light sauce.

1 Preheat the oven to 450°F. Place the turkey in a roasting pan; you can place stuffing under its breastbone if you like; if you want crisp stuffing, however, add it to the pan (or bake it separately) when about 30 minutes of cooking time remains.

2 Brush the turkey with oil, butter, or stock if you like and season it with salt and pepper to taste. Place it in the oven. Roast for 40 to 60 minutes, depending on size, basting with the pan juices (or a little more chicken stock) every 15 minutes or so, then begin checking for doneness every few minutes with an instant-read thermometer. The turkey is ready when the thermometer reads 155 degrees. Let the turkey rest for 5 to 10 minutes (during which time its internal temperature will rise to about 160 degrees) before carving and serving.

WINE A light red, like Beaujolais or a minor Pinot Noir.

SERVE WITH You can turn this into a typical Thanksgiving feast with the usual array of side dishes. If you're making it as a simple weeknight meal, serve it with mashed potatoes and a cooked vegetable, like Roasted Asparagus with Parmesan (page 166) or Green Beans with Lemon (page 168).

SMALLER TURKEY BREASTS OF ABOUT three pounds are perfectly adequate for a party of four or so, while the larger ones—they're available in sizes of six pounds and even more—can be counted on to serve about ten, especially if you make a few side dishes.

IF YOU PREFER THE KIND of soggy dressing that results from stuffing it into the turkey, just pile it under the cavity formed by the breast bone.

IT'S WORTH NOTING THAT ALTHOUGH basting a turkey gives the skin added flavor, it does nothing to maintain interior moisture, let alone add to it; the only way to ensure moist meat is to avoid overcooking. So if one of your guests is on a serious low-fat diet—an increasingly common occurrence—baste with chicken stock or not at all.

FINALLY, FOR SAFETY, THE USDA recommends roasting white-meat poultry to 170 degrees, at which point it will be unpalatably dry (especially when you consider that the internal temperature typically rises at least five degrees during the resting period). Should you choose to do this, I strongly recommend that you serve the turkey with plenty of gravy. I stop the cooking at a lower temperature (see Step 2) and have never regretted it.

Herb Roasted Turkey Breast: Increase the melted butter, oil, or stock to ¼ cup, and combine with ¼ cup parsley, along with a mixture of other fresh herbs, such as tarragon (about a teaspoon), dill (about a tablespoon), celery or fennel leaves (a tablespoon or more), or other fresh herbs. Baste and roast as above.

Turkey Tonnato

TIME: 2 hours, largely unattended
MAKES: 4 servings

Vitello tonnato is a northern Italian specialty in which cold roast veal is marinated and then served in a creamy, mayonnaise-like sauce of canned tuna. (It didn't sound good the first time I heard of it either, but the combination is magical, and it's one of the great picnic dishes of all time.) But what a hassle: To make it, you begin by roasting a piece of leg of veal, or eye of veal round, or some other hard-to-find, fairly expensive cut. Then you chill it, slice it, layer it with the sauce, and chill it again.

Turkey, it seems to me, is enough like veal to use as a substitute. And then I had a brainstorm: Why not buy the highest-quality deli turkey I could find, thick-sliced? The next time I was in the supermarket I bought some and gave it a try, and the results were great. I felt a slight tinge of guilt for not roasting the turkey breast from scratch, but I quickly got over it when I tasted the results.

1 cup fresh Mayonnaise (page 192) or bottled mayonnaise

2 tablespoons capers

6 anchovy fillets, minced

1 can (6 ounces) tuna packed in olive oil

¼ cup olive oil, more or less

Salt and freshly ground black pepper

Eight ¼- to ⅜-inch-thick slices white-meat turkey

Minced parsley for garnish

1 Combine the mayonnaise with the capers, anchovies, and tuna. Thin with olive oil (or hot water) to achieve a creamy consistency. Taste and add salt and pepper as necessary.

2 Make a thin layer of sauce on a platter; cover with 4 turkey slices, then more sauce, then the remaining turkey slices, and finally more sauce. Cover and refrigerate for at least 2 hours and up to 2 days; serve cold or at room temperature, garnished with parsley.

WINE A light red or even rosé.

SERVE WITH This is a good dish for a cold meal, so best served with bread and salads.

MOST DELI COUNTERS HAVE SEVERAL grades of turkey; buy the best you can find, and get it sliced it really thick, at least ¼-inch.

IF YOU'VE NEVER MADE MAYONNAISE yourself, this is the place to begin.

Almost any spin you can put on mayonnaise will work here. Try folding in about ¼ cup of:

■ chopped pitted olives (black, green, or a combination)

■ minced shallots or scallions

■ chopped cornichons or other pickles

■ minced red bell pepper

■ or garnish the dish with more capers or chopped olives

Pan-fried Duck

TIME: 60 minutes
MAKES: 4 servings

What probably keeps you from cooking duck more frequently—most people reserve it for special occasions—isn't that you don't like it, but that the roasting methods that efficiently rid duck of its thick layer of fat take a great deal of time and a fair amount of attention. (Not that roast duck is impossible; see page 130.) But here's a method that takes less than an hour and results in a crisp bird from which nearly all of the fat has been rendered. It's accomplished by the simple procedure of cutting up the duck, then cooking it, covered, on top of the stove. Served hot or at room temperature, the bird is crisp, tender, and far more flavorful than any chicken.

One 5- to 6-pound duck
Salt and freshly ground black pepper
3 garlic cloves, optional

Several sprigs of fresh thyme, optional

1 Cut the duck into 6 or 8 serving pieces, reserving the wing tips, back, and neck for the stockpot. (Cut the gizzard into slices and cook it along with the duck if you like; reserve the liver for another use.) Place the duck, skin side down, in a 12-inch skillet, and sprinkle it liberally with salt and pepper. Add the garlic and a few thyme sprigs if you like and turn the heat to medium-high. When the duck begins to sizzle, cover the skillet and turn the heat to medium.

2 After 15 minutes, turn the duck and season the skin side. After 15 more minutes, uncover the skillet and turn the heat back to medium-high. Cook the duck, turning as necessary, so that it browns nicely on both sides; this will take another 15 minutes.

3 Serve hot or at room temperature. Strip some of the leaves from the remaining thyme sprigs and use them as a garnish if you want.

WINE Here's a simple dish that can stand up well to a great wine, the best, richest red you can lay your hands on. An inexpensive, soft Rioja would do well also.

SERVE WITH Crispy sautéed or creamy mashed potatoes would be great with this, as would a salad or any cooked vegetable.

BY CUTTING THE BIRD into serving pieces, you readily expose large chunks of surface fat, and can easily trim them. If you have never cut up a raw duck, you will be relieved to know that it is nearly identical to cutting up a chicken.

IF YOU WOULD LIKE TO RENDER the trimmed duck fat—it's great for cooking—cut it into pieces and cook it in a skillet, slowly, until all the fat has liquefied and the bits of skin have become crisp. Drain and eat the crispy bits, and refrigerate the fat; it will keep for weeks.

Soy Duck: Rub the duck with salt, pepper, 1 tablespoon soy sauce, and 1 tablespoon dry sherry before placing it in the pan. When it is done, garnish with minced fresh ginger or minced cilantro leaves.

Roast Duck in One Hour

TIME: About an hour
MAKES: 2 to 4 servings

What turns people off to roasting duck—its thick layer of subcutaneous fat—is actually its best feature, one that makes it a nearly foolproof dish, absolutely suitable for a weeknight meal. The fat keeps the meat juicy even when it's well done—a distinct advantage because the breast is best medium-rare, but the legs must be cooked through, or nearly so, to be palatable.

In fact, duck is so difficult to roast badly that all experienced cooks seem to claim their procedure is the best. Having tried many methods, I can say that the results are all about the same. So I usually rely upon the one presented here, which I believe is the easiest way to guarantee a succulent but beautifully browned bird.

One 4- to 5-pound duck
Freshly ground black pepper

¼ cup soy sauce, more or less

1 Preheat the oven to 450°F. Discard the neck and giblets or keep them for another use; remove excess fat from the duck's cavity.

2 Place the duck, breast side down (wings up), on a rack in a roasting pan; add water to come to just below the rack. Sprinkle with pepper and brush with a little soy sauce.

3 Roast for 30 minutes, undisturbed. Prick the back all over with the point of a sharp knife, then flip the bird onto its back. Sprinkle with pepper and brush with soy sauce again. Add a little more water to the bottom of the pan if the juices are spattering (carefully—you don't want to get water on the duck).

4 Roast 20 minutes, prick the breast all over with the point of a knife, and brush with soy sauce. Roast 10 minutes; brush with soy sauce. Roast another 5 or 10 minutes if necessary, or until the duck is a glorious brown all over and an instant-read thermometer inserted into the thigh measures at least 155 degrees. Let rest for 5 minutes before carving and serving.

WINE Roast duck can stand up well to good red wine, from a rich red to something soft like Rioja.

SERVE WITH An assortment of lightly cooked vegetables is ideal, along with potatoes however you like them.

ALL THAT SPATTERING FAT can make a mess of your oven. The solution is simple: Keep a thin layer of water in the roasting pan. The fat drips into it and stays there. (You'll need a rack to elevate the duck, but you should be using one anyway.)

TO ACHIEVE A UNIFORMLY BROWN color, brush the roasting duck with soy sauce, which works like a charm.

A DUCK IS A LITTLE MORE complicated to carve than a chicken. The best thing to do is cut on either side of the rib cage to remove two boneless breast halves, then cut the legs from the carcass. The rest is for picking.

THERE IS A BASIC CHALLENGE of having enough to go around; a roast duck can easily be finished by two people. If you want to serve four, roast two, or plan on a lot of side dishes.

■ Follow the general rules for making a reduction sauce (page 188), and you can sauce this duck however you like (chicken stock and green peppercorns are always good; orange juice is classic). Just make sure to drain nearly all of the fat first. You can flavor the duck in a variety of ways while it's roasting:

■ Put a whole lemon, cut in half, in the cavity while the bird roasts; squeeze the juice from the cooked lemon over the bird after you carve it.

■ Stuff the bird with a few sprigs of thyme or parsley.

■ Keep the pan juices moist with water or stock, and cook, along with the duck, a few chopped leeks, carrots, celery stalks, and/or onions.

■ There is another method for roasting duck, one that is more work but gives somewhat better results: First, steam the duck on a rack over simmering water until it is nearly cooked, about forty-five minutes. Then chill it for up to a day; finally, roast it on a rack in a roasting pan at 400°F for about thirty minutes until the skin is crisp.

The Minimalist's Thanksgiving Turkey

(Fastest Bread Stuffing, Sherry Reduction Sauce)

TIME: 2 hours 30 minutes

MAKES: At least 12 servings (with leftovers)

12-pound turkey

1 recipe Bread Stuffing (below)

Salt and freshly ground black pepper

One Thanksgiving, I vowed to minimize everything: time, number of ingredients, and, most of all, work. My goal was to buy all the food with one trip to the store and prepare the entire feast in the time it took to roast my twelve-pound turkey—less than three hours. The results are close to a traditional Thanksgiving dinner, a full-fledged feast for twelve with more food than anyone could possibly finish.

The stuffing was inspired by a clever recipe from the late Pierre Franey; you can make it and stuff the bird in less time than it takes to preheat the oven. The sauce relies on pan drippings, but is finished with nothing more than water, good sherry, and butter; it's made in ten minutes or so, while the turkey rests before carving.

1 Preheat the oven to 500°F. Rinse the turkey and remove the giblets; save the liver to make the stuffing. Loosely pack the turkey cavity with the stuffing, then tie the legs together to enclose the vent.

2 Place the turkey on a rack in a large roasting pan. Add ½ cup water to the bottom of the pan along with the turkey neck, gizzard, and any other trimmings. Place in the oven, legs first.

3 Roast 20 to 30 minutes, or until the top begins to brown, then turn the heat down to 350 degrees. Continue to roast, checking every 30 minutes or so; if the top threatens to brown too much, lay a piece of aluminum foil directly onto it. If the bottom dries out, add water, about ½ cup at a time. The turkey is done when an instant-read thermometer inserted into the thickest part of the thigh measures 165 degrees. If, when the turkey is nearly done, the top is not browned enough, turn the heat back up to 425 degrees for the last 20 to 30 minutes of cooking.

4 Remove the turkey from the oven. Take the bird off the rack and make Sherry Reduction Sauce, page 134, while the bird rests (let it sit for about 20 minutes before carving).

WINE A fruity white, like Riesling, Chenin Blanc, or Gewürztraminer, or a light red like Beaujolais.

SERVE WITH Serve this with oven-browned sweet potatoes, Green Beans with Lemon (page 168), cranberry-orange relish, and Pear and Gorgonzola Green Salad (page 26).

TIME: 15 minutes, plus turkey-cooking time

MAKES: 12 servings

Fastest Bread Stuffing

6 tablespoons butter

3 chicken livers, about ¼ pound, or an equivalent amount of turkey liver

1 cup chopped parsley leaves

Salt and freshly ground black pepper

8 slices good day- or two-day-old white bread, crusts trimmed

1 Chop together (by hand or in a small food processor) the butter, livers, and parsley; season with salt and pepper to taste.

2 Spread half of the mixture on 4 of the bread slices; use the remaining bread to make 4 sandwiches. Spread the remaining mixture on the outside of the sandwiches. Cut each of the sandwiches into 6 pieces.

3 Stuff the turkey as described above.

Keys To SUCCESS

THE TURKEY GETS A HIGH-HEAT boost at the beginning so the bird gets a fast start. This ensures browning and keeps roasting time well under three hours. It works.

Sherry Reduction Sauce

1½ cups Amontillado or
  Oloroso sherry

3 tablespoons butter, optional

Salt and freshly ground black
  pepper

1 Remove the giblets and pour off all but a tablespoon of
  the fat from the turkey's roasting pan; leave as many of
  the solids and as much of the dark liquid behind as possible. Place the roasting pan over two burners and turn
  the heat to high.

2 Add the sherry and cook, stirring and scraping all the
  brown bits off the bottom of the pan, until the liquid has
  reduced by about half, 5 minutes or so.

3 Add 3 cups water (or stock if you have it) and bring to a
  boil, stirring all the while. Turn the heat to medium and
  simmer for about 5 minutes.

4 Stir in the optional butter and, when it melts, salt and
  pepper to taste. Keep warm until ready to serve. Strain
  before serving if desired.

STEAK WITH BUTTER AND GINGER SAUCE

NEGIMA: JAPANESE BEEF-SCALLION ROLLS

PERFECT GRILLED STEAK

OSSO BUCO

BRAISED VEAL BREAST WITH MUSHROOMS

CRISP ROASTED RACK OF LAMB

BRAISED AND GRILLED LAMB SHANKS

GRILLED LAMB RIBS

BRAISED PORK WITH TURNIPS

ROAST PORK WITH FENNEL-ORANGE COMPOTE

ROAST PORK WITH APPLESAUCE

SAUSAGE WITH GRAPES

THE MINIMALIST'S CHOUCROUTE

Meat

Steak with Butter and Ginger Sauce

TIME: 20 minutes

MAKES: 4 servings

Cooking steak simply, with good results, is easy as long as you have an outdoor grill (see the recipe on page 140). But sometimes it's winter, or perhaps you don't own a grill, and cooking a steak in the broiler or oven usually means sacrificing a good crust; using the stovetop just sets off the smoke detector. There is, however, an alternative: Sear the steak quickly, then remove it from the pan before building a quick sauce in which you can finish cooking the meat. This reduces smoke while increasing flavor, and is such a good technique, with so many options, that you might even eschew the grill just to do it this way.

1 to 1½ pounds boneless top blade, skirt, sirloin or rib-eye, ¾ inch thick or less

1½ tablespoons butter

1 tablespoon minced fresh ginger

2 tablespoons soy sauce

1 Preheat a large, heavy skillet over medium-high heat until it begins to smoke. Add the steaks and cook until nicely browned, 1 to 2 minutes. Turn and brown the other side, another minute or two. Remove the skillet from the heat and the steaks to a plate.

2 When the skillet has cooled slightly, return it to the stove over medium heat. Add the butter and, when it melts, the ginger. About 30 seconds later, add the soy sauce and stir to blend. Return the steaks to the skillet, along with any of their accumulated juices. Turn the heat to medium and cook the steaks for a total of about 4 minutes, turning three or four times. (If at any time the pan threatens to dry out entirely, add a couple of tablespoons of water.) At this point, the steaks will be medium-rare; cook for a little longer if you like, and serve, with the pan juices spooned over.

WINE Red, but nothing too fancy: Chianti, Zinfandel, or inexpensive Cabernet.

SERVE WITH Not bad with rice, this steak preparation is equally at home with bread or potatoes; use your judgment depending on the seasonings you choose. A green salad is great.

IT ISN'T NECESSARY to use butter in this preparation, but a small amount—there is little more than a teaspoon per person in the recipe—adds not only creaminess but also flavor.

THE TECHNIQUE IS NOT DEPENDENT on butter, ginger, or soy. As you can see from the variations, each of these three ingredients can be swapped, varied, even omitted, until the dish has nothing in common with the original recipe except the steak and the procedure used to cook it.

IT'S BEST TO USE fairly thin steaks here. Judging the doneness of thicker ones can be tricky, and inevitably the sauce evaporates before the meat is cooked through. The ideal setup for four people is four small, boneless steaks, cut from the top blade, sirloin, or rib. But two larger steaks will work nearly as well, as long as they're thin.

By varying the ingredients around the steak, you can give this recipe any number of different flavors. For example:

- Substitute extra virgin olive oil for the butter, garlic for the ginger, and fresh lemon juice for the soy sauce; or stay with the butter, but use garlic or shallots and a few leaves of tarragon instead of the ginger, and vinegar in place of the soy sauce.

- Substitute minced garlic or any member of the onion family for the ginger, or use minced lemongrass or anchovies; whole capers or finely chopped mushrooms are also good.

- You can omit the butter entirely or substitute any oil you like. Extra virgin olive oil and peanut oil are the most distinctive.

- In place of the soy sauce, use red wine, fresh lemon or lime juice, vinegar, or nam pla (fish sauce). Start with about a tablespoon (¼ cup in the case of wine) and add more to taste. Or thin with water.

- Add any minced herbs you like to the sauce, at about the same time you return the meat to the skillet.

Negima: Japanese Beef-Scallion Rolls

TIME: 30 minutes

MAKES: 4 servings

Wrapping one food with another is familiar, especially if meat, cheese, or vegetables comprise the filling—think of ravioli, stuffed cabbage, or egg rolls. Making meat the wrapping is a nice role reversal, a neat twist that is extraordinary enough to allow a simple preparation to wow a crowd. Such is the case with the Japanese negima, in which beef is wrapped around chives or scallions, then brushed with soy sauce and grilled.

8 thin slices of beef, chicken, veal, or pork, each about 3 inches wide and 5 to 6 inches long (about 1¼ pounds)

¼ cup soy sauce

Green parts from about 2 dozen scallions

1 Preheat a grill or broiler; the fire should be quite hot.
2 Place the meat between two layers of wax paper or plastic wrap and pound it gently so that it is about ⅛ inch thick. Brush one side of each piece of meat with a little soy sauce.
3 Cut the scallions into lengths about the same width as the meat and place a small bundle of them at one of the narrow ends of each slice. Roll the long way, securing the roll with a toothpick or two. (You can prepare the rolls in advance up to this point; cover and refrigerate for up to 2 hours before proceeding.) Brush the exterior of the roll with a little more soy sauce.
4 Grill until brown on all sides, a total of about 6 minutes for chicken, 4 to 5 minutes for pork or veal, 4 minutes or less for beef.

WINE Very light red—like Beaujolais, slightly chilled—or crisp white: dry Sauvignon Blanc or full-bodied Chardonnay.

SERVE WITH A good fried rice dish, or one of stir-fried noodles (like Rice Noodles with Basil, page 58), would be ideal, but grilled vegetables brushed with soy sauce would also be nice. Or both.

CHICKEN, VEAL, AND PORK are easier to work with than beef, because the cuts of beef that supermarkets most frequently slice thin are from the round, which is not only tough but relatively tasteless. If you prod your supermarket butcher you may get slices of sirloin cut thin enough. But chicken, veal, and pork are routinely sold as thin cutlets, which can be made even thinner with a little gentle pounding.

YOU CAN USE store-bought teriyaki sauce here, but I prefer the less complex but purer flavor of plain soy sauce. There are other options as well; see "With Minimal Effort."

Scallion greens are a wonderful filling, but chives work well, as do:

■ Small amounts of lightly cooked, chopped spinach or chard

■ Cooked, chopped shiitake (or other) mushrooms

■ Julienned and lightly cooked carrots

■ Parboiled asparagus spears

As alternatives to soy sauce, you can use Asian fish sauce (nam pla or nuoc mam), Chinese hoisin sauce, or premade teriyaki sauce.

Perfect Grilled Steak

TIME: 30 minutes

MAKES: 4 servings

There are just two reasons for marinating before grilling: to add flavor and promote browning and crispness. Neither of these requires much time, although dunking the meat or fish for a few minutes in what is best labeled a grilling sauce may contribute to a slightly greater penetration of flavor. (On the other hand, if you really have no time at all, simply smear the food with the sauce as it's going on the grill.)

Which flavor to add is a matter of taste. My favorite is soy sauce; I love its taste, and it always seems to contribute exactly the right amount of saltiness. Its natural complements are garlic and ginger; for best flavor, each of these should be fresh rather than powdered. And promoting browning is easy: Anything with sugar browns quickly—often too quickly, as you know if you've ever slathered a piece of chicken with barbecue sauce before grilling it.

¼ cup soy sauce

1 teaspoon peeled and minced fresh ginger

½ teaspoon peeled and minced garlic

1 tablespoon honey, molasses, or hoisin sauce

Freshly ground black pepper

Juice of ½ lime

16 to 24 ounces boneless steak (such as rib eye, skirt, or strip), or 24 to 32 ounces bone-in steak (such as rib eye or T-bone)

1 Start a charcoal or wood fire, or preheat a gas grill; the fire should be hot, and the rack no more than 4 inches from the heat source. Mix together the first 6 ingredients; taste and add more of anything you like. Turn the steak in the sauce once or twice, then let it sit in the sauce until the grill is hot.

2 Turn the steak one more time, then place on the grill; spoon any remaining sauce over it. For rare, grill about 3 minutes per side for steak under an inch thick. For larger or more well-done steak, increase the time slightly.

WINE A sturdy red, like Chateauneuf du Pape or something else from the south of France, or a good California Cabernet.

SERVE WITH Grilled vegetables if you can manage it; a hunk of bread; some salad (Grilled Bread Salad, page 24, is great). But after all, it's steak; you can serve it with nearly anything.

SINCE THERE IS SWEETENER HERE, you also need some acid, to balance it; lime goes best with soy, but almost any acidic liquid will do, from lemon juice to white vinegar.

THERE IS A SAFETY ISSUE HERE: Marinade that is applied to raw food should not be brushed on during the last few minutes of cooking, nor should it be used as a sauce unless it is boiled for a few minutes. And, as always, marinade brushes and other utensils that are used with raw food should not be used near the end of cooking.

This combination—soy and spices for flavor; honey for browning, body, and sweetness; lime for acidity—perfectly enhances not only steak but burgers, boneless chicken breasts or thighs, tuna, and swordfish. Longer-cooking meats, such as bone-in chicken, should be cooked to within 10 minutes of doneness before basting with the sauce.

There are many other ingredients that can contribute to this basic sauce to make it somewhat more complex in flavor. Add too many at once, however, and you run the risk of muddying the flavor. But try:

- 1 teaspoon to 1 tablespoon mustard

- about a teaspoon sesame or other roasted-nut oil

- about a tablespoon of peanut butter or tahini (sesame paste). (Some sesame seeds or finely chopped peanuts are good, too.)

- some onion, scallion, or shallot

- a tablespoon or more horseradish, or a teaspoon wasabi powder

- some minced zest of lemon, lime, or orange

- some minced cilantro, about a tablespoon, plus more for garnish

- up to a tablespoon ground cumin, or coriander (up to a teaspoon), or a combination

- some minced jalapeño, crushed red chiles, or Tabasco or other hot sauce to taste

- about a tablespoon Worcestershire or fish sauce (nuoc mam or nam pla, sold in most Asian markets)

Osso Buco

There is no promise of speed here: Osso buco takes time. But this classic Italian dish of glorious, marrow-filled veal shanks (the name means "bone with hole"), braised until they are fork-tender, is dead easy to make and requires a total of no more than fifteen or twenty minutes of attention during its two hours or so of cooking. And it holds well enough overnight so that 90 percent of the process can be accomplished while you're watching television the night before you serve the dish.

1 tablespoon olive oil

4 center-cut slices veal shank, 2 pounds or more

Salt and freshly ground black pepper

3 to 4 garlic cloves, lightly smashed and peeled

4 anchovy fillets

1 cup dry white wine, chicken or beef stock, or water

2 teaspoons butter, optional

1 Heat a large, deep skillet over medium-high heat for a couple of minutes. Add the oil, swirl it around, and pour out any excess. Add the veal and cook until nicely browned on the first side (for even browning, you can rotate the shanks, but try not to disturb them too much), about 5 minutes. Turn and brown the other side.

2 When the second side is just about completely browned, sprinkle the shanks with a little salt and pepper and add the garlic and anchovies to the pan. Cook, stirring a little, until the anchovies dissolve and the garlic browns, about 2 minutes. Add the liquid and let it bubble away for about a minute.

3 Turn the heat to low and cover the skillet. Five minutes later, check to see that the mixture is simmering—just a few bubbles appearing at once—and adjust the heat accordingly. Cook until the meat is very tender and pulling away from the bone, at least 90 minutes and

WINE A rich, good red like Barolo, a not-too-dry Cabernet, or Rioja.

SERVE WITH Traditionally, risotto with Parmesan (*risotto alla Milanese*), and you cannot do much better, though Parmesan Cups with Orzo Risotto, page 60, are great (even without the cups). For some reason, I also love cooked carrots with osso buco.

probably somewhat more; turn the veal every half hour or so. (When the meat is tender you may turn off the heat and refrigerate the dish for up to 24 hours; reheat gently before proceeding.)

4 Remove the meat to a warm platter and turn the heat to high. Boil the sauce until it becomes thick and glossy, about 5 minutes. Stir in the butter if you like and serve the meat with the sauce spooned over it.

Traditionally, osso buco is served with a condiment known as gremolata. To make it, mix together 1 tablespoon minced lemon zest, 2 tablespoons minced fresh parsley leaves, and ¼ to 1 teaspoon minced garlic (remember that this will not be cooked, so go easy on the garlic).

Osso Buco with Vegetables: Omit the anchovy; the garlic is optional. Instead, cook 1 cup chopped onions; 1 chopped celery stalk; 2 medium carrots, peeled and chopped; and a couple of sprigs of thyme (or about ½ teaspoon dried thyme) in the skillet over medium heat, after browning the meat. When the vegetables are tender, about 10 minutes, add the liquid and proceed as above.

Osso Buco with Tomatoes: Add about 2 cups chopped tomatoes (canned are fine; drain them first) to the skillet along with the liquid. Proceed as above. This version is excellent with about ½ cup roughly chopped basil added during the last few minutes of cooking, and some minced basil as a garnish.

Keys To SUCCESS

TRY TO BUY SLICES OF SHANK taken from the center, about one and one half inches thick. The slices from the narrow end have very little meat on them; those from the thick end contain little or no marrow. Center cuts give you the best of both worlds.

AS USUAL, the richest sauce results from using good-quality stock. But two hours of cooking veal shanks—which are, after all, veal bones—creates a very nice stock with no work, so I never hesitate to make osso buco with white wine or even water.

COOKING THE PAN JUICES over high heat for a few minutes after the meat is done results in a glossy, silken pan sauce that can barely be bettered, though the hedonist will stir in a couple of teaspoons of butter to enhance the sauce even further.

Braised Veal Breast with Mushrooms

TIME: At least 90 minutes, largely unattended

MAKES: 4 or more servings

Few slow-cooked foods are as rewarding as beef brisket, which at its best is tender, juicy, and flavorful. Doing it right takes so long—my favorite recipe is a twelve-hour job—that, at least in my house, a brisket is made only annually, or even less often than that. That's why I regret that I didn't make my "discovery" of veal brisket sooner. It had just never occurred to me until recently that you could get a delicious, tender, relatively quick-cooking form of brisket by removing the bones from a breast of veal.

Unfortunately, boneless breast of veal—which can also be called veal brisket is rarely sold that way. But any butcher (and, yes, this includes virtually every supermarket butcher) can quickly remove the bones from a veal breast and present you with a flat, boneless, relatively compact cut that contains little fat and becomes tender in less than two hours of unattended cooking.

1 ounce dried mushrooms, such as shiitakes, porcini, or a combination

One 2- to 3-pound boneless veal breast

½ cup white wine

Salt and freshly ground black pepper

1 tablespoon butter, optional

1 Reconstitute the mushrooms by covering them with very hot water. Turn the heat under a 12-inch skillet to medium-high and let the pan sit for a minute. Add the veal and brown it on both sides, turning once, for a total of about 6 minutes.

2 Remove the meat to a plate and turn the heat to medium. Add the mushrooms and about ½ cup of their liquid (strained, if necessary, to remove sediment) along with the wine. Bring to a boil and cook for about 30 seconds, then return the veal to the skillet. Season with salt and pepper, turn the heat to low, and cover.

3 Cook for 60 to 90 minutes, turning once or twice during that period and checking now and then to make sure the liquid is bubbling slowly; adjust the heat accordingly.

4 When the meat is tender, remove it to a cutting board. Turn the heat under the liquid in the skillet to high and reduce it to a thick, saucy consistency. Stir in the butter if you like and keep warm. Carve the meat against the grain into ¼-inch-thick slices and serve with the sauce.

WINE Red, and hearty: A Côtes du Rhône or decent Cabernet would be great.

SERVE WITH This dish cries for buttered noodles, but bread, rice, or potatoes would also be fine. Cooked carrots or any other simple vegetable dish would complete the meal.

ASK THE BUTCHER TO START WITH A PIECE OF BREAST that weighs four to six pounds. The yield is about half that, a piece of boneless meat of two or three pounds that will easily fit in a large skillet. (Consider asking the butcher for the bones, too—you're paying for them, and they are among the best for stock making.)

I LIKE TO USE DRIED MUSHROOMS, largely because of their convenience and intensity of flavor, but you can substitute about a half-pound of fresh mushrooms if you prefer; see With Minimal Effort.

Veal Brisket with Fresh Mushrooms: Brown the veal as above, then take at least ½ pound fresh mushrooms, button or other. Slice them, then cook them over medium-high heat in 2 tablespoons olive oil or butter, preferably with a couple of crushed, peeled garlic cloves and a few sprigs of thyme, until tender, about 15 minutes. Proceed as above, adding ½ cup water in place of the mushroom-cooking liquid.

Veal Brisket with Bacon and Onions: Render about ¼ pound cubed bacon, preferably cut from a slab, over medium heat, stirring, until crisp. Then remove the bacon pieces with a slotted spoon. Brown the veal in the fat, as above. Remove the veal and cook 1½ cups chopped onions (or about 15 pearl onions) in the fat over medium heat until nicely browned. Proceed as above, beginning by adding the mushrooms and their liquid.

■ For a richer sauce, substitute ½ cup good chicken or beef stock for the wine.

■ For a much richer sauce, stir in up to 4 tablespoons of butter, a bit at a time, at the end of cooking.

■ You can also cook the veal with fresh vegetables: After the meat has simmered for about 30 minutes, add 15 peeled pearl onions (or about 1½ cups chopped onions), 1 cup chopped carrots, ½ cup chopped celery, or any combination of vegetables that you like. You will probably have to add another ½ cup or so of liquid.

Crisp Roasted Rack of Lamb

TIME: 30 minutes
MAKES: 4 servings

Rack of lamb—a row of unseparated rib chops—has been a restaurant feature for so long that many people assume there is some trick to cooking it. But there is not. You trim the rack of excess fat and roast it at high heat. Salt and pepper are good seasonings, there are a number of quick tricks for adding flavor to the exterior, and you can of course make a quick reduction sauce before serving it. But these are options and by my standards unnecessary: The distinctive flavor of true lamb is an uncommonly fine treat.

2 racks of lamb, each about 1½ pounds

Salt and freshly ground black pepper

1 Preheat the oven to 500°F. Strip most of the surface fat from the lamb (your butcher may already have done this). Cut between the ribs, almost down to the meaty eye. Divide each rack in half down the middle, sprinkle with salt and pepper to taste, and place in a roasting pan.

2 Roast for 15 minutes, then insert a meat thermometer straight in from one end into the meatiest part. If it reads 125 degrees or more, remove the lamb immediately. If it reads 120 degrees or less, put the lamb back for about 5 minutes. Remove and let sit for 5 minutes; this will give you medium- to medium-rare lamb on the outer ribs, medium-rare to rare in the center. Cook a little longer for more doneness. Serve, separating the ribs by cutting down straight through them.

WINE Break out the best red you have: Bordeaux or other good Cabernet is the classic.

SERVE WITH Crisp potatoes, whether roasted or sautéed, are ideal. An elegant vegetable gratin would be great (see, for example, Roasted Asparagus with Parmesan, page 166), but so would a simply steamed vegetable or a salad.

GETTING TRUE LAMB IS PART OF THE PROBLEM; the mild flavor of baby lamb has a more universal appeal than the gamier flavor of older meat. Make sure to tell the butcher you want a rack that weighs less than two pounds.

BECAUSE MANY RESTAURANTS OFFER A WHOLE RACK as a serving (six to eight ribs!), many people believe that to be a standard serving size. But there are almost no circumstances where even a small rack will not serve two people; a larger rack can accommodate three and sometimes four. To serve more, just cook two racks at a time; they will fit comfortably side by side in most roasting pans. I like to cut each rack in half before roasting. This makes for slightly more uniform cooking, and also relieves you from separating each rack into individual ribs before serving.

THE ROASTING ITSELF IS CHILD'S PLAY. Your oven should be hot (it should also be well insulated, because high heat produces smoke). Cut the rack most of the way down between the ribs so that more meat is exposed to intense heat and therefore becomes crisp. ("Frenching" the ribs—scraping the meat off the bones to leave them naked and neater in appearance— is counterproductive; the crisp meat on the bones is one of the joys of rack of lamb.) Unless you're highly experienced, the most reliable method of judging doneness is with an instant-read thermometer; 125 degrees in the center will give you medium-rare meat.

Spice-Rubbed Rack of Lamb: Rub a teaspoon or more of your favorite spice rub—curry powder, chili powder, or anything else you find appealing—into the meaty side of the racks before roasting.

Rack of Lamb Persillade: Combine 2 tablespoons olive oil, 1 cup plain bread crumbs, 1 small peeled garlic clove, and about ½ cup fresh parsley leaves in a small food processor (or chop by hand). Process until minced, then rub into the meaty side of the racks before roasting.

Rack of Lamb with Red Wine or Port Sauce: When the lamb is done roasting, remove it to a warm platter. Pour off all but a tablespoon of its fat and place the roasting pan on a burner (or two burners, if it is big) over high heat. Add 1 cup good red wine or port and cook, stirring and scraping, until the liquid is reduced to about ⅓ cup. Add any of the liquid that has accumulated around the lamb and stir. Season to taste, then spoon a little of this over each serving of rib.

Braised and Grilled Lamb Shanks

TIME: At least 2½ hours, largely unattended

MAKES: 4 servings

Why do so many recipes have you brown lamb shanks and other tough meats, when the subsequent two or more hours of braising needed to make them tender breaks down the lovely, crisp crust that the browning process created? The simple answer is that browning creates complex flavors—and it's true. But browning meat at the beginning of cooking creates a legion of hot, flying drops of fat, often accompanied by minor burns and a huge mess. Which explains why many people avoid it entirely.

Here's one solution: Cook lamb shanks (or short ribs, or any other really tough cut of meat on the bone) for a long time in liquid, without initial browning. The result is complexity of flavor, supreme tenderness, and little hassle. When the braising is done, grill or broil the shanks, which will give them the ultimate crust. The braising liquid serves as a succulent sauce.

4 lamb shanks, each about 1 pound

1 cup port or red wine

8 garlic cloves (don't bother to peel them)

Salt and freshly ground black pepper

1 teaspoon red wine vinegar or fresh lemon juice, or to taste

1 Combine the lamb shanks, port or wine, and garlic in a skillet just large enough to hold the shanks. Turn the heat to high and bring to a boil; cover and turn down the heat so that the mixture simmers gently. Cook, turning about every 30 minutes, until the shanks are tender and a lovely mahogany color, at least 2 hours and more likely longer.

2 Remove the shanks and strain the sauce. If time allows, refrigerate both separately; skim the fat from the top of the sauce. Preheat a charcoal or gas grill, or the broiler; the rack should be 4 to 6 inches from the heat source, and the fire hot.

3 Grill or broil the shanks until nicely browned all over, sprinkling them with salt and pepper to taste and turning as necessary; total cooking time will be about 15 minutes. Meanwhile, reheat the sauce gently; season it with salt and pepper, then add the vinegar or lemon juice. Taste and add more seasoning if needed. Serve the shanks with the sauce.

WINE Red and rich; Rioja would be ideal.

SERVE WITH Rice or bread, for sure—you need something for the sauce. If you're grilling, do some vegetables. If not, a steamed vegetable or salad.

A COMBINATION OF PORT AND GARLIC provides plenty of flavor, but if you want to add a few aromatic vegetables to the broth, like carrots, onions, and celery, they'll certainly make a contribution.

IT PAYS TO ARRANGE YOUR SCHEDULE to make this slow-cooked dish in leisurely fashion. For example, braise the shanks the night before serving them, while you're cooking something else or even out of the kitchen entirely. They need occasional turning (I suggest every thirty minutes, but fifteen minutes more or less between turnings won't matter), but no more attention than that. When they're done, refrigerate meat and sauce separately; well wrapped, they'll keep perfectly for two or three days. This allows you to skim the fat from the sauce before reheating; the shanks will reheat in the time it takes to brown them.

■ You can treat short ribs in exactly the same fashion; cooking time may be a little shorter. The ribs are done when the meat falls from the bone.

Anise-Flavored Lamb Shanks (or Short Ribs): Braise the meat in a mixture of ¼ cup soy sauce, 1 cup water, 5 thin slices fresh ginger, 5 whole star anise, 4 garlic cloves, and 1 tablespoon sugar. Proceed as above, finishing the sauce with rice or white wine vinegar.

Lamb Shanks with Carrots: Follow the original recipe, using red wine (the carrots are so sweet that port would be overkill). After 1 hour of cooking, add 2 cups peeled carrots, cut into chunks. Proceed as above; you may brown the carrots lightly or leave them in the sauce.

Grilled Lamb Ribs

TIME: 30 minutes
MAKES: 4 servings

If you don't see lamb ribs in your supermarket, the chances are that they're being tossed. Both demand and profit are evidently so slim that they are not worth processing and putting out in the case. Which is a shame, because next to pork (spare) ribs, lamb ribs are the best down-and-dirty grill item I know. They're also the cheapest. Where I live, it's hard to pay more than a dollar a pound for them.

4 to 5 pounds lamb breast, cut into ribs

Salt and freshly ground black pepper

¼ cup honey, orange marmalade, or maple syrup

¼ cup Dijon mustard

1 small onion, peeled

1 Start a charcoal or wood fire or preheat a gas grill or broiler; the fire should only be moderately hot and the rack should be at least 4 inches from the heat source. Bring a large pot of water to the boil; salt it. Put in the lamb and simmer for 10 minutes.

2 Drain the ribs. Grill or broil them for about 10 minutes, turning once or twice and sprinkling them with a little salt and pepper. Meanwhile, combine the honey, mustard, and onion in a blender and whiz until smooth.

3 When the ribs begin to brown, brush them with the sauce and continue to cook, watching carefully so they do not catch fire. When they are brown and crisp all over—a matter of no more than 10 or, at the most, 15 minutes—remove from the grill and serve.

WINE Red and rough, something from the south of France, or central Italy (Chianti is good); Beaujolais is also good, lightly chilled if you like.

SERVE WITH You can't go wrong with grilled vegetables, especially since you have the grill on already. Mashed potatoes are good, too, and you'll want a light, crisp salad.

LIKE PORK RIBS, lamb ribs require special treatment while grilling. They are loaded with fat, which, if not handled properly, will melt onto the coals (or open flame of a gas grill) and catch fire. To avoid this, par-boil the ribs, just for ten minutes or so, to render enough of the fat so that it doesn't catch fire when you put the ribs on the grill.

ANY BRUSHING SAUCE OR SPICE RUB you like is suitable here. My choice is a sweet but pungent amalgam of raw onion, strong mustard, and honey, marmalade, or maple syrup.

You can make a fast, more typical, barbecue sauce like this: Combine a cup of ketchup with a tablespoon each of Worcestershire sauce and chili powder; ¼ cup each red wine vinegar and minced onion; a clove of garlic, minced; and salt and pepper. Combine this mixture in a saucepan and cook over medium-low heat, stirring occasionally, until warm, about 10 minutes. Taste and adjust seasoning, then use as above.

Braised Pork with Turnips

TIME: 60 minutes
MAKES: 4 servings

This is a classic spring or fall dish, times when you can get good, fresh turnips but don't mind long, slow cooking. Here, turnips and pork are both browned for perfect color and then simmered in a little liquid until tender. The pork should be boneless, and should contain at least a little fat to keep it moist; shoulder is the best cut, but loin is good, too. You may use either white turnips (the purple-topped variety is most common) or yellow rutabagas, usually considered coarser in flavor than true turnips but in truth equally good. White wine or chicken stock is the best liquid, because each contributes some flavor of its own to the dish, but the pork and turnips simmer long enough to produce good-tasting juice even if you use water.

1 tablespoon neutral oil, such as canola

1 tablespoon butter (or use all oil)

1½ pounds boneless pork shoulder or loin, trimmed of excess fat and cut into 1- to 1½-inch chunks

1½ pounds purple-topped turnips or rutabaga, peeled and cut into 1-inch chunks

¾ cup white wine, chicken stock, or water

Salt and freshly ground black pepper

2 tablespoons minced fresh lovage, celery leaves, or parsley, optional

1 Place a 12-inch skillet, preferably nonstick, over medium-high heat and let sit for at least a minute. Add the oil and butter. When the butter foam subsides or the oil is hot, add the pork, a few chunks at a time. When it is all in the skillet, turn the heat to high. Cook for about 5 minutes, undisturbed, until the pork is nicely browned on one side. Turn each piece, return the heat to medium-high, and cook about 3 minutes more.

2 Add the turnip chunks and shake the skillet so that the pork and turnips are all sitting in one layer or nearly so. Cook for another 3 or 4 minutes, or until the turnips begin to brown. Add the liquid and stir once or twice. Add salt and pepper to taste and half the optional lovage, turn the heat to medium-low, and cover the skillet.

3 Cook, stirring every 10 minutes, until both pork and turnips are quite tender, about 30 minutes. Remove the

WINE Pinot Noir or other not-too-heavy red, or a good, potent Chardonnay.

SERVE WITH With bread or rice, this is pretty much a complete meal, but you might want a salad for contrast as well.

cover and raise the heat to medium-high; boil the liquid until it is reduced to a syrupy glaze. Taste and add more salt and pepper if necessary, then garnish with the remaining herb if you like and serve.

Keys To SUCCESS

GARDENERS OR THOSE WITH READY ACCESS to greenmarkets can use lovage, whose intense, celerylike flavor shouts freshness, but celery leaves or parsley make a similar contribution.

THE TECHNIQUE FOR THIS DISH IS SIMPLE, although it's always worth pointing out that meat does not brown automatically: It requires high heat and constant contact with the cooking surface. To get a nice brown surface on the meat, you must preheat the skillet for at least a minute, then allow the butter and/or oil to become hot, not crowd the meat (one and a half pounds of cubed meat will just about fit in the bottom of a twelve-inch skillet), and allow the meat to sear, undisturbed, for a few minutes before turning. These are cubes of meat, so theoretically you could brown six sides of each piece, but just make sure that the first side browns well and that the second is on its way to being browned before adding the turnips. The turnips themselves are so high in natural sugars that they brown almost instantly, and continue to gain color as they braise.

Creamy Pork with Turnips: In the final step, remove the pork and turnips to a warm platter. Do not quite reduce the liquid to a glaze; when there is about ½ cup left, reduce the heat to low, stir in 1 cup sour or sweet cream, and slowly bring back to a boil over medium heat. Stir the pork and turnips back into the sauce; garnish and serve, preferably over rice.

Pork and Turnips with Mustard: You can do this in combination with the above variation if you like. Stir 1 tablespoon Dijon mustard, or more to taste, into the finished sauce. Heat through and serve.

Roast Pork with Fennel-Orange Compote

TIME: 45 minutes
MAKES: 4 servings

It isn't often you can combine a few winter staples and create a novel, fresh-tasting dish that is easily varied, stands on its own, or forms the base for a variety of other foods. Yet a simple mélange of fennel and orange does all of these things, and without a lot of effort. Take some slices of boneless pork, for example, marinate them briefly in olive oil, lemon juice, garlic, salt, and pepper, pan-roast them, then serve them on a bed of the compote: The mingled juices are sheer delight. (I've presented the recipe that way here, but it is easy to cook the fennel-orange combination on its own.) Similarly, the compote works nicely as a bed for simple roasted cod, sautéed duck breast, and grilled chicken.

4 boneless pork chops, 1 to 1½ pounds

Salt and freshly ground black pepper

4 tablespoons extra virgin olive oil

Juice of 1 lemon

1 fennel bulb, 1 pound or more

2 navel oranges, peeled

1 medium onion, peeled

1 tablespoon fresh rosemary or 1 teaspoon dried rosemary

1½ cups orange juice

1 Sprinkle the pork chops with salt and pepper to taste and marinate them on a plate with 2 tablespoons of the olive oil and the lemon juice. Preheat the oven to 500 degrees.

2 Trim the fennel, reserving some of the dill-like fronds. Cut the fennel, oranges, and onion into ⅛- to ¼-inch-thick slices.

3 Place the remaining olive oil in an 8-inch skillet or a saucepan that is at least 4 inches deep. Place half the fennel in the skillet, then top with half the orange, the onion, and the rosemary. Sprinkle with salt and pepper, then top with the remaining fennel and orange. Pour in the juice, and add more salt and pepper.

4 Bring to a boil on top of the stove and cook over fairly lively heat, pressing the solids down into the liquid from time to time. When the mixture is no longer swimming in juice but not yet dry—about 20 minutes—it is done. Hold it at minimum heat while you finish the pork chops.

5 Just before you judge the compote to be done, heat an ovenproof skillet over high heat for 3 or 4 minutes. Add

WINE White, fruity but dry: Alsatian Riesling or Gewürztraminer would be ideal.

SERVE WITH Mashed or crispy potatoes would be best, along with a light salad.

the pork chops with their marinade and immediately transfer the skillet to the oven (if you have a powerful vent, you can pan-grill the chops on top of the stove). Roast 2 minutes, then turn and roast another 2 to 3 minutes, or until the chops are done.

6 Serve the chops on a bed of the compote. Mince the reserved fennel fronds and use as a garnish.

Keys To SUCCESS

THERE ISN'T MUCH TECHNIQUE to speak of here; you'll know the dish is done when the orange juice bubbles become scarce. Just make sure not to cook the compote entirely dry; the orange juice sauce is a nice touch.

With MINIMAL Effort

■ Substitute grapefruit for the oranges, or add the juice of a lemon or a lime to the mix.

■ Vary the herb. Classic Western European herbs such as rosemary, thyme, tarragon, and parsley are all naturals, but cilantro or finely minced lemongrass also adds a nice touch.

■ Add finely minced fresh ginger along with some garlic and soy sauce. A teaspoon or so of roasted sesame oil finishes the compote nicely. Substitute peanut oil for the olive oil if you have it, or use a neutral oil such as canola.

■ Any meat, like steak, can be cooked like the pork. Grilled chicken, on or off the bone, works well, as does sautéed duck breast. You can also make the dish with fish: Try roasted delicate fillets, such as cod or red snapper; or grilled shrimp; or swordfish, tuna, or salmon steaks.

Roast Pork with Applesauce

TIME: 60 minutes

MAKES: 4 servings

Spreading a roast with a sweet coating—apricot jam comes to mind—serves a dual purpose. It adds sweetness, an element of flavor not often found in savory dishes, and the sugar encourages browning. But the results are often too sweet. So I decided to experiment with alternative coatings for a small roast of pork—one that would cook quickly enough to be considered for weeknight dinners—and settled on applesauce, which has a not-too-obvious benefit. Because applesauce doesn't contain nearly the same percentage of sugar as jam, more of it can be used without overwhelming the meat with sweetness, and the thicker coating protects the meat and keeps it moist. This is important, because the superlean pork sold in supermarkets almost inexorably dries out as it cooks.

One 1½- to 2-pound pork loin

2 cups applesauce, preferably unsweetened

Salt and freshly ground black pepper

1 Preheat the oven to 500°F; set the oven rack as close to the top of the oven as is practical (take the thickness of the roast into account). Meanwhile, put the applesauce in a fine strainer over a bowl or in the skink to allow excess liquid to drain. Line a roasting pan with a double thickness of aluminum foil and brush the foil with a little oil.

2 When the oven is hot, sprinkle the roast with salt and pepper, then spread an even layer of the applesauce all over it, using up all the applesauce. Sprinkle with a little more salt and pepper and roast, checking every 15 minutes or so to make sure the applesauce doesn't burn. It's fine if it darkens and browns, or even turns dark brown, as long as the top doesn't blacken.

3 Begin checking the pork with an instant-read thermometer after 45 minutes. When the internal temperature reaches 155 degrees, remove the meat from the oven. Let it rest 5 minutes before carving. Serve the sliced meat with any accumulated juices.

WINE Red and hearty, though not necessarily expensive: Something from southern France, or a deep California Cabernet or Zinfandel, or Rioja.

SERVE WITH You might serve roast pork with applesauce, but that's out here. Mashed or home-fried potatoes are great, along with any cooked vegetable or a salad.

UNSWEETENED APPLESAUCE DOES NOT BROWN AS QUICKLY or as well as jam; to counter this, drain some of the liquid from the applesauce (this can be done while the oven is preheating), and roast the pork at an extremely high oven temperature.

BONELESS PORK IS FINE HERE (the applesauce keeps it from overcooking), but steer clear of tenderloin, which is so lean that it seems to dry out just by being in the vicinity of the oven. The lean end of the loin is nearly as bad, but a roast taken from the loin's center is acceptable. Best of all is a cut from the shoulder end of the loin, which contains a higher percentage of the darker, moister meat.

A WORD ABOUT CLEANUP, or minimizing it: The small amounts of applesauce that drip off the pork onto the surface of the roasting pan will burn and stick; removing this mess is more work than the entire cooking process. You can avoid this by coating the bottom of the roasting pan with a double layer of aluminum foil, lightly brushed with a tiny bit of oil.

Roast Pork with Jam or Marmalade: This is the original version, which some will prefer: Substitute 1 cup apricot jam or orange marmalade for the applesauce; warm it over low heat, stirring in 1 tablespoon fresh lemon juice to thin it slightly. Proceed as above.

Sausage with Grapes

TIME: 30 minutes
MAKES: 4 servings

Although I was told this dish—beautifully browned sausages nestled on a bed of grapes in varying stages of doneness, some lightly browned, some collapsed, some whole and nearly raw—is Umbrian in origin, it seems as if many workers of the land who produced sausages and picked grapes would have created this, even if by accident, no matter where they lived. It is an often overlooked recipe in cookbooks, perhaps because there's almost nothing to it—there is neither the challenge nor the trendiness of sausages and polenta, for example. In any case, the wonderful marriage is incredibly easy to produce and easily worked into anyone's repertoire. With good bread and a salad, you've got a great weeknight meal in about half an hour.

1 to 1½ pounds fresh Italian sausage

4 cups seedless grapes

2 teaspoons balsamic vinegar or fresh lemon juice, or to taste

1 Place the sausages in a 10- or 12-inch skillet and turn the heat to medium. Cook the sausages, turning from time to time, until they are nicely browned, about 15 minutes. When they are brown all over, prick each sausage in a few places with a thin-bladed knife and cook for 5 minutes more.

2 Remove the sausages to a warm platter. If more than a tablespoon or two of fat remains in the pan, remove the excess. Add the grapes and turn the heat to medium-high. Cook, stirring occasionally, until some of the grapes collapse. Add the vinegar or lemon juice, stir, and turn off the heat. Serve the sausages nestled in the grapes and their juices.

WINE Chianti or another light but tannic red.

SERVE WITH Mashed potatoes, bread, salad—some or all. You could precede the sausages with a light pasta dish, like Spaghetti with Fresh Tomato Sauce, page 50.

BROWN THE SAUSAGE OVER MODERATE HEAT to reduce spattering. To minimize mess even further, don't prick the sausages to release their fat until they are almost cooked; they will brown perfectly even in a completely dry skillet.

BEFORE COOKING THE GRAPES, you might drain off the excess fat. These days, however, many sausages are quite lean, and even a pound releases only a tablespoon of fat during cooking—the minimum you need for the grapes. As the grapes cook, they release some of their liquid, which combines with the fat to form a lovely brown sauce. Because standard seedless grapes are somewhat one-dimensional in flavor and lacking in acidity, this sauce needs a minuscule amount of balsamic vinegar or lemon juice to balance it. That's it—even salt and pepper are unnecessary.

Sausage with Grapes and Pan Gravy: Before adding the grapes, add 1 cup white wine or chicken stock to the skillet. Raise the heat to high and cook, stirring, until the liquid is reduced by about half. Stir in the grapes and proceed as above. Serve with mashed potatoes (see below) or bread.

Bangers-and-Mash, Italian Style: Boil 1½ to 2 pounds peeled potatoes in water to cover until soft; drain, reserving some of the cooking liquid. While the potatoes are hot, mash them with ½ teaspoon minced garlic, 2 tablespoons extra virgin olive oil, and enough of the reserved cooking liquid to make them smooth. Season to taste with salt and pepper. Reheat if necessary and serve with the sausages and grapes. Especially good with the preceding variation.

The Minimalist's Choucroute

TIME: About 2 hours, largely unattended

MAKES: 6 servings

In its homeland of Alsace, *choucroute garnie* is no more special than a frank and sauerkraut, with which it has much in common. But while the French treat this archetypically hearty combination of sauerkraut, spices, wine, and smoked meats as common fare, here it has become the province of restaurants. In any case, choucroute is a flexible combination of wintertime staples, the perfect cold-weather dish, featuring sauerkraut cooked in a little goose fat (or duck fat, or lard) and wine, then "garnished"—this is some garnish—with a variety of candidly heavy meats, some smoked, some fresh or salted. The seasonings are simple, usually little more than juniper and onion, but the meat and cabbage are assertive enough so that the dish demands strong mustard.

3 pounds sauerkraut

1 large onion, chopped

10 juniper berries

2 cups dry white wine, preferably Alsatian Riesling

1 pound slab bacon, in one piece

1 pound kielbasa or similar dark sausage

3 bratwursts or similar "white" sausage

3 smoked loin pork chops

Salt and freshly ground black pepper

1 Wash the sauerkraut and drain it well. Combine it with the onion, juniper berries, and wine in a large skillet or broad pot and add enough water to come about two-thirds of the way up the side of the sauerkraut (in some pots, the wine may provide enough liquid). Turn the heat to high and bring to a boil.

2 Turn down the heat and nestle the bacon in the sauerkraut. Cover and cook 60 minutes, then add the sausages and pork chops. Re-cover and cook another 30 minutes. The sauerkraut should be tender but retain some crunch; cook another 15 minutes if necessary, then taste and season with salt and pepper to taste.

3 To serve, cut the meat into pieces and serve it on a platter with the sauerkraut along with hot mustard.

WINE Alsatian white: Pinot Blanc, Riesling, or Gewürztraminer.

SERVE WITH Note the variations in With Minimal Effort, many of which make this into a one-pot meal. Serve with rye bread or pumpernickel.

GOOD SAUERKRAUT DOES NOT COME IN CANS, but is sold fresh from barrels, or in plastic. It should contain no more than cabbage and salt—beyond that, the less the better.

■ Add several tablespoons of duck fat or lard to the simmering sauerkraut (a traditional addition).

■ Use any sausages you like, including those made from chicken, veal, turkey, or seafood.

■ Add 12 small potatoes to the pot when about 45 minutes remain to cook.

■ Add 2 to 3 peeled, cored, and grated apples to the sauerkraut when about 15 minutes of cooking remains.

■ Stir 2 tablespoons kirsch into the sauerkraut about 5 minutes before serving.

GRILLED ASPARAGUS WITH LEMON DRESSING

ROASTED ASPARAGUS WITH PARMESAN

GREEN BEANS WITH LEMON

BEET ROESTI WITH ROSEMARY

FENNEL GRATIN

TENDER SPINACH, CRISP-SHALLOTS

PIQUILLO PEPPERS WITH SHIITAKES AND SPINACH

QUICK SCALLION PANCAKES

SPANISH TORTILLA

Vegetables

Grilled Asparagus
with Lemon Dressing

TIME: 20 minutes
MAKES: 4 servings

Much as I like steamed asparagus, by mid-April I'm ready to move on to other ways of preparing this ancient symbol of spring. My first alternative is always the grill, another element of cooking that makes its appearance this time of year, and one that treats asparagus perfectly. I love the earthy, charred flavor added by the grill, a flavor that can also be achieved with stove-top pan-grilling, which combines high heat and a dry, heavy skillet.

1½ to 2 pounds large asparagus

Olive oil as needed, about 2 tablespoons

Salt and freshly ground black pepper

Juice of 3 lemons

2 tablespoons minced shallots or scallions

¼ cup minced fresh parsley leaves

1 Snap off the woody ends of the asparagus; most spears will break naturally an inch or two above the bottom. Peel the stalks up to the flower bud. Meanwhile, start a charcoal fire or preheat a gas grill; if you're cooking inside, preheat a cast-iron or other heavy skillet over medium-high heat until it smokes.

2 To grill the asparagus, toss them with about 1 tablespoon of the oil, mixing with your hands until they're coated. Season well with salt and pepper to taste. Grill until tender and browned in spots, turning once or twice, a total of 5 to 10 minutes.

To pan-grill the asparagus, do not oil or season them. Just toss them in the hot skillet and cook until tender, turning the individual spears as they brown, 5 to 10 minutes. Remove as they finish, and season with salt and pepper.

WINE White and crisp, like Sauvignon Blanc or Pinot Grigio.

SERVE WITH If you are grilling, the simplest thing to do is to pick a sturdy fish that can be grilled without falling apart, such as tuna, monkfish, or swordfish. Any of these can be lightly oiled, seasoned, and slapped on a grill, to be cooked in about the same time as the asparagus. Use the same dressing for the fish. Or try Grilled Fish the Mediterranean Way, page 74.

3 Mix together the lemon juice and shallots, then stir in enough olive oil to add a little body and take the edge off the sharpness of the lemon; the mixture should still be quite strong. Season it with salt and plenty of black pepper and stir in the parsley. Serve the asparagus hot or at room temperature. Spoon the sauce over all.

Asparagus with Soy-Ginger Dressing: Combine ¼ cup soy sauce with ½ teaspoon minced garlic, 1 teaspoon minced fresh ginger, ½ teaspoon sugar, 2 teaspoons rice or other mild vinegar, and a few drops of sesame oil. Serve over the asparagus.

■ Serve the asparagus with any vinaigrette (pages 186–187) you like.

Keys To SUCCESS

FOR THIS PREPARATION, you want thick spears of asparagus, which remain tender and moist inside while their exteriors brown. Those that weigh an ounce or two each—that is, eight to sixteen per pound—are the best. The only disadvantage to thick asparagus is that they must be peeled before cooking in order to remove the relatively tough skin; use a vegetable peeler or paring knife.

Roasted Asparagus with Parmesan

TIME: 25 minutes
MAKES: 4 servings

There are two distinct advantages to pencil-thin asparagus that seem to get overlooked. One is that it requires no peeling, because its outer sheath is far more tender than that of its thick cousin. And the other is that it cooks much faster. This is especially important when you turn to methods other than boiling or steaming—most notably roasting. What I like to do is roast thin spears until they're just about tender, then top them with a foolproof two-ingredient topping: coarse bread crumbs and Parmesan cheese. Run that under the broiler, and you get roasted asparagus with a crunchy, high-impact crust.

1 thick slice good bread, about 1 ounce

1 small chunk Parmesan cheese, about 1 ounce

1½ pounds thin asparagus, more or less

3 tablespoons butter, extra virgin olive oil, or a combination

Salt and freshly ground black pepper

1 Preheat the oven to 500°F; while it's preheating, put the bread in there, and check it frequently until it is lightly toasted and dry. Coarsely grind or grate the bread and Parmesan together (a small food processor is perfect for this)—if possible, keep the crumbs from becoming as small as commercial bread crumbs.

2 Rinse the asparagus and break off their woody bottoms. Lay them in a baking dish that will accommodate them in two or three layers. Toss with bits of the butter and/or oil, sprinkle lightly with salt and pepper, and place in the oven.

3 Roast for 5 minutes, then shake the pan to redistribute the butter or oil. Roast another 5 minutes, then test the asparagus for doneness by piercing a spear with the point of a sharp knife; it is done when the knife enters the asparagus but still meets a little resistance. You can prepare the recipe in advance up to this point up to a couple of hours before serving; allow the asparagus to sit at room temperature during that time.

WINE Any dry white.

SERVE WITH This flavorful side dish will overshadow nearly anything you serve on the center of the plate, so keep it simple—grilled or broiled meat or fish, perhaps with some lemon.

4 Turn on the broiler and place the rack as close as possible to the heating element. Spread the bread crumbs and Parmesan over the asparagus, then carefully brown the top—it will only take a minute or two—and serve hot or at room temperature.

Keys To SUCCESS

ALTHOUGH I DO THINK real Parmesan is best—especially if you combine it with butter—pecorino or other hard sheep's cheese does a nice job. Use coarse bread crumbs if possible; they might look slightly less attractive, but will give you more crunch.

KEEP YOUR EYE ON THE DISH while it's under the broiler—the time needed there is only a minute or two.

With MINIMAL Effort

Roasted Asparagus with Garlic: Forget the topping; just toss the asparagus with 1 tablespoon minced garlic at the same time as you add the butter or olive oil.

Roasted Asparagus with Soy and Sesame: Use 1 tablespoon peanut oil in place of the olive oil or butter. Halfway through the roasting, add 1 tablespoon soy sauce to the asparagus. Top with about 2 tablespoons sesame seeds; run under the broiler until they begin to pop, about 1 minute. Finish with a sprinkling of soy sauce, just a teaspoon or two.

Green Beans with Lemon

There is one technique for cooking vegetables that is almost infallible, and works for almost every vegetable you can think of. You precook the vegetables—this is something you can do twenty minutes before you eat or twenty-four hours in advance—and then chill them. At the last minute, you reheat them in butter or oil (or, if you're especially fat-conscious, a dry nonstick skillet). That's it. The advantages are numerous. You can precook a lot of vegetables at once, using the same water for each. You can store them, and cook as much as you need when you need it. You can finish the cooking in five minutes. And the technique is foolproof. I use green beans as an example, but this is as close to a generic recipe as there is; it will work with any vegetable that is suitable for cooking in water—beets, potatoes, turnips, broccoli, greens, cauliflower, fennel, snow peas, shell peas, carrots, or cabbage, to name just a few.

1 pound green beans

1 to 2 tablespoons extra virgin olive oil or butter, or a combination

1 lemon

1 Bring a large pot of water to a boil and salt it; add the beans and cook until bright green and tender, about 5 minutes. Do not overcook.

2 Drain the beans, then plunge them into a large bowl filled with ice water to stop the cooking. When they're cool, drain again. Store, covered and refrigerated, for up to a couple of days, or proceed.

3 Zest the lemon and julienne or mince the zest. Juice the lemon. Place the oil and/or butter in a large skillet and turn the heat to medium-high. Add the beans and cook, tossing or stirring, until they are hot and glazed, 3 to 5 minutes. Toss in a serving bowl with the lemon juice, top with the zest, and serve.

WINE Determined by the main course.

SERVE WITH This is a classic side dish, useful in accompanying almost any main course.

THE ONLY PRECAUTION HERE is not to overcook. You want the beans (or any other vegetable you cook using this technique) to be just short of perfectly cooked when you remove them from the boiling water and plunge them into the cold water.

There's little you cannot do with precooked vegetables, but here are some good ideas:

■ Sprinkle the cooked vegetable with toasted slivered nuts, bread crumbs, or sesame seeds.

■ Add a teaspoon or so of garlic to the butter and/or oil as it is cooking; or use a tablespoon or two of minced shallot, onion, or scallion.

■ Add a tablespoon or more of soy sauce to the finished vegetable, with or without the lemon.

■ Substitute lime juice or vinegar for the lemon juice. Or use any vinaigrette (pages 186-187) as a dressing.

■ Toss the vegetable with a couple of table-spoons of minced mild herbs—parsley, dill, basil, or chervil, for example—as it is heating.

Beet Roesti with Rosemary

TIME: 30 minutes
MAKES: 4 to 6 servings

Beets are so sweet that most recipes counter with acidity or other sharp flavors. But showcasing the sweetness of beets is an attractive alternative, wonderfully exploited in this roesti, a dish created about ten years ago by Michael Romano, the long-standing chef at Manhattan's Union Square Café. It's a thick beet pancake, cooked slowly on both sides until the beet sugars caramelize and a crunchy, sweet crust forms that, I swear, is reminiscent of crème brûlée. A touch of rosemary added to the mix does not diminish the sweetness at all, but simply adds another dimension.

2 pounds beets (about 3 very large or 4 to 6 medium)

2 teaspoons coarsely chopped fresh rosemary

Salt and freshly ground black pepper

½ cup flour

2 tablespoons butter or olive oil

Minced parsley or a few rosemary leaves for garnish

1 Trim the beets and peel them as you would potatoes; grate them in a food processor or by hand. Begin preheating a 12-inch nonstick skillet over medium heat.

2 Toss the grated beets in a bowl with the rosemary, salt, and pepper. Add about half the flour; toss well, add the rest of the flour, then toss again.

3 Place the butter in the skillet and heat until it begins to turn nut-brown. (If using oil, just heat a minute or so.) Scrape the beet mixture into the skillet, and press it down with a spatula to form a round. With the heat at medium to medium-high—the pancake should be gently sizzling—cook, shaking the pan occasionally, until the bottom of the beet cake is nicely crisp, 8 to 10 minutes. Slide the cake out onto a plate, top with another plate, invert the two plates, and return the cake to the pan. Continue to cook, adjusting the heat if necessary, until the second side is browned, another 10 minutes or so. Garnish, cut into wedges, and serve hot or at room temperature.

WINE Should be determined by the main course.

SERVE WITH A stunning side dish for hearty roasted or braised meat dishes, this also makes a good centerpiece for a light meal.

BEETS BLEED, AS YOU KNOW. Peel them over the sink, and wash the grater or food processor as soon as you're done with it, and you won't have any serious consequences. Still, you might wear an apron.

THE GRATING DISK of a food processor processes the beets quickly and easily, but a box grater works well also.

THE ROESTI MUST BE cooked in a nonstick skillet, preferably a large one measuring twelve inches across. (If you only have a ten-inch skillet, decrease the amount of beets in the recipe from two pounds to one and a half pounds; the quantity given for other ingredients can remain the same.)

KEEP THE HEAT MODERATE: Too-quick cooking will burn the sugary outside of the pancake while leaving the inside raw.

Beet Salad with Vinaigrette: You don't need to cook the grated beets; simply toss them, raw, with any vinaigrette (pages 186-187). Given their sweetness, a strong, harsh vinaigrette, with a high percentage of vinegar, is best.

Fennel Gratin

This is a good, almost universal technique for vegetables, an honest, simple gratin with a topping of just a couple of ingredients. Since one of them is rich, flavorful blue cheese, it doesn't even include butter. My vegetable of choice here is fennel—an underappreciated and almost always available bulb—but you could put this topping on almost any vegetable.

1 fennel bulb, about 1 pound

½ cup coarse bread crumbs

¼ cup crumbled blue cheese

Freshly ground black pepper

1 Preheat the oven to 400°F. Bring a pot of water to a boil.

2 Trim the fennel, then cut into about ¼-inch-thick slices and cook in the boiling water until just tender, less than 5 minutes. Drain and layer in a shallow baking dish. (You can also drain the vegetables, then stop their cooking by plunging them into ice water, then drain again. In this manner you can finish the cooking up to a day or two later; increase the baking time to 20 minutes.)

3 Top the fennel with the bread crumbs, then with the cheese; season all with pepper to taste (hold off on salt, because the cheese is salty). Place in the oven until the cheese melts, about 10 minutes.

4 Run the baking dish under the broiler until the top browns, checking every 30 seconds. Serve hot or at room temperature.

WINE A good, solid red—Cabernet or one of the Rhône varietals—would probably be best.

SERVE WITH A side dish, for sure, but one that can dominate the table; serve it with plain broiled chicken or fish.

THE BREAD CRUMBS ARE BEST when freshly made from good but slightly stale bread; coarse bread crumbs, such as those made in a food processor, are infinitely preferable to the finer store-bought variety.

FOR THE CHEESE, you can use Gorgonzola, the soft Italian cheese; bleu d'Auvergne, a mild cheese from France; Maytag blue, the premier domestic variety; Stilton, the classic English blue; and Roquefort, which is made from sheep's milk. All are good, but my preferences are for the stronger cheeses, such as Roquefort and Maytag.

■ Almost any vegetable will work here; some must be parboiled (see Green Beans with Lemon, page 168): green beans, broccoli, cauliflower, leeks, celery, etc. Some need not be (see Roast Asparagus with Parmesan, page 166): thin asparagus, zucchini, sliced tomatoes.

■ The flavoring can be changed by varying the cheese. Or toss a couple of tablespoons of minced parsley in with the bread crumbs, or a tiny bit (½ teaspoon or so) of minced garlic.

Tender Spinach, Crisp Shallots

TIME: 30 minutes
MAKES: 4 servings

More people eat greens because they think they should rather than because they actually like them, but there are a number of ways to make greens more appealing. First and foremost is to give them the treatment described in detail for green beans on page 168. You simmer the greens—spinach will take about a minute, collards a good ten—then drain them and toss them with seasonings and oil or butter. Then you might try a topping of crisp-fried shallots, which by themselves are irresistible and which, when combined with tender greens, create an alluring contrast in flavor and texture. Like the greens themselves, the shallots can be prepared well in advance. When you're ready to eat, you just reheat the greens and sprinkle them with the shallots.

1 cup or more neutral oil, such as grapeseed, canola, or corn

6 to 8 large shallots (about 6 ounces), peeled and thinly sliced

1 pound spinach, washed and trimmed

Salt and freshly ground black pepper

2 tablespoons fresh lemon juice

1 Place the oil in a small-to-medium saucepan or narrow, deep skillet; the oil should be at least an inch deep. Turn the heat to high and wait a couple of minutes, then add the shallots and cook, adjusting the heat so that the bubbling is vigorous but not explosive. Cook, stirring, until the shallots begin to darken, 10 to 15 minutes. As soon as they turn golden brown, remove them immediately with a slotted spoon—be careful, because overcooking at this point will burn the shallots. Drain the shallots on paper towels and sprinkle with salt and pepper; they'll keep for a couple of hours this way.

2 Meanwhile, bring a large pot of water to a boil and salt it. When it is ready, add the spinach and cook until it wilts, about 1 minute. Remove the spinach with a strainer or slotted spoon and plunge it into a large bowl filled with ice water to stop the cooking. When it's cool, drain and chop. (You can store the spinach, covered and refrigerated, for up to a couple of days if you like.)

3 Take 1 tablespoon of the shallot oil and place it in a skillet; turn the heat to medium-high. Turn the spinach into

WINE Depending on the center-of-the-plate preparation, a full-bodied Chardonnay is a likely candidate.

SERVE WITH Use this as a bed for simply broiled chicken or fish and it becomes a whole meal.

this skillet and cook, stirring frequently and breaking up any clumps, until the spinach is hot, about 5 minutes. Season with salt and pepper, add the lemon juice, and serve, topped with the crisp shallots.

Keys To SUCCESS

THE SHALLOTS MUST BE thinly sliced, and this is the perfect occasion to use a mandoline if you have one. If you do not, just peel, then slice them as thinly as you can, using a small, sharp knife.

THIS PREPARATION ALSO serves as a good introduction to deep-frying, because the watchful eye can readily and infallibly detect when the shallots are ready—they turn brown. At that moment, they must be removed from the heat immediately or they will burn. The deliciously flavored oil should be strained and stored in the refrigerator; it can be used in vinaigrettes (pages 186-187), or in cooking.

With MINIMAL Effort

■ You can use any leafy green you like here. Some, like collards and kale, will take up to 10 minutes to soften in the boiling water; just keep testing for doneness (sampling) until you're satisfied that they're tender. (Thick stems of ¼ inch or more will take even longer; start them in the water a few minutes before adding the greens.)

■ And, of course, the crisp-fried shallots can be used as a garnish for almost any dish.

Piquillo Peppers with Shiitakes and Spinach

TIME: About 30 minutes
MAKES: 4 servings

Pimientos del piquillo—piquillo peppers— are the brilliant crimson, cone-shaped peppers from Navarre, a region of western Spain. You couldn't bioengineer a better shape for stuffing, and there's no preparation involved, because piquillo peppers are sold only in cans or bottles. All of this adds up to a terrific "new" ingredient for home cooks. Here they're stuffed with shiitakes and spinach, an easy preparation. But you can use almost any stuffing you like, as noted in With Minimal Effort. Or you can sauté the piquillos unstuffed; they're great that way.

¼ cup extra virgin olive oil

2 garlic cloves, peeled and sliced

1 dried hot red chile

2 cups stemmed shiitake mushrooms, thinly sliced or chopped

1 cup cooked spinach, squeezed dry and chopped

Salt and freshly ground black pepper

12 piquillo peppers

1 Place the olive oil in a large skillet, turn the heat to medium, and add the garlic and chile. Cook, stirring occasionally, until the garlic browns lightly, about 5 minutes. Remove the chile and add the shiitakes. Cook, stirring occasionally, until the shiitakes release their liquid and become tender, about 10 minutes. Stir in the spinach and season to taste.

2 Stuff each of the peppers with a portion of this mixture. Serve at room temperature or warm gently in a 250°F oven for about 15 minutes.

WINE Rioja or another soft, rich red.

SERVE WITH Generally, you'd serve these as a main course for a light meal, with salad and bread.

THE BEST PIQUILLOS are from a town called Lodosa, and are so labeled. They are harvested by hand, then roasted over wood and hand-peeled—no water is allowed to touch them, for this would wash away some of the essential flavors—and canned or bottled with no other ingredients. This regal treatment makes top-quality peppers expensive, about fifteen dollars per pound, but there are alternatives: Some Lodosa peppers are roasted over gas, some have citric acid added as a mild preservative, and there are also piquillo-style peppers from other parts of Spain.

YOU CAN PURCHASE piquillo peppers at many specialty food retailers, or (as of this writing) by mail from Formaggio Kitchen in Cambridge, MA (888-212-3224) or 86-17 Northern Boulevard Corp., Jackson Heights, NY (718-779-4971).

Sautéed Piquillos: Place 2 tablespoons extra virgin olive oil in a large skillet, turn the heat to medium-low, and add 2 teaspoons peeled and slivered garlic. Cook, shaking the pan occasionally, until the garlic turns light brown, about 5 minutes. Add 8 to 12 piquillo peppers and cook just until the peppers begin to change color on the bottom; turn and repeat. Season and serve hot or at room temperature drizzled, if you like, with a little more olive oil and some sherry vinegar.

Piquillos with Anchovies: No cooking here, just place an anchovy fillet in each pepper and drizzle with olive oil, then serve.

Piquillo Bruschetta: Toast a few rounds of good bread; rub each with a cut clove of garlic and top with a piquillo, or if the bread is small, half a piquillo. Drizzle with olive oil and serve.

Other stuffing suggestions for piquillo peppers:

■ Spinach or other greens sautéed with raisins and pine nuts

■ Cooked and chopped tender fish fillets (such as cod or salmon), tossed with chopped tomatoes and a little oil and vinegar

■ Stewed and chopped or shredded meat

■ Rice bound with a little mayonnaise and chopped shrimp or chicken (good served cold)

Quick Scallion Pancakes

TIME: About 30 minutes
MAKES: 4 servings

These are simpler than traditional scallion pancakes, which are made from a breadlike dough, and they taste more like scallions, because the "liquid" is scallion puree. The flavor is great, the preparation time is cut to about twenty minutes, and the texture is that of a vegetable fritter.

4 bunches scallions or spring onions, about 1 pound

1 egg

1 teaspoon soy sauce

½ cup flour

Salt and freshly ground black pepper

Peanut, canola, or olive oil as needed

1 Bring a medium pot of salted water to a boil while you trim the scallions. Roughly chop about three-quarters of them, and mince the remainder.

2 Add the larger portion of scallions to the water and cook about 5 minutes, or until tender. Drain, reserving about ½ cup of the cooking liquid. Puree the cooked scallions in a blender, adding just enough of the cooking liquid to allow the machine to do its work.

3 Mix the puree with the egg and soy sauce, then gently stir in the flour until blended; add pepper and the reserved minced scallions. Film a nonstick or well-seasoned skillet with oil and turn the heat to medium-high. Drop the batter by the tablespoon or ¼ cup and cook the pancakes for about 2 minutes per side, or until lightly browned. If necessary, the pancakes can be kept warm in a 200°F oven for about 30 minutes.

WINE Will depend on the center-of-the-plate preparation.

SERVE WITH These are good not only as a side dish, but as a platform for stews and juicy roasts, like Spicy Chicken with Lemongrass and Lime (page 110). And although I still associate them with Asian-flavored dishes, if you omit the optional soy sauce, they're a perfect accompaniment to braised foods that use European seasonings.

BECAUSE THE BATTER is so delicate, it's better to make these as individual pancakes, which are easy to turn, than as one big cake.

I USE PEANUT OIL for this recipe, but that's only because I associate it with soy sauce. If you omit the soy you can use any vegetable oil you like, even good olive oil.

The same method can be used to make pancakes with many members of the onion family, especially shallots and spring onions (which look like scallions on steroids). There are also some quick additions to the batter to vary the pancakes:

- Toasted sesame seeds, about 1 tablespoon

- Roughly chopped peanuts, about 2 tablespoons

- Minced chives, added along with the uncooked scallions, about ¼ cup

- Cayenne to taste

- Minced fresh ginger, a tablespoon or so

Spanish Tortilla

The Spanish tortilla has nothing in common with the Mexican tortilla except its name, which comes from the Latin *torta*—a round cake. In its most basic form, the Spanish tortilla is a potato-and-egg frittata, or omelet, which derives most of its flavor from olive oil. Although the ingredients are simple and minimal, when made correctly—and there is a straightforward but very definite series of techniques involved—this tortilla is wonderfully juicy. And because it is better at room temperature than hot, it can and in fact should be made in advance. (How much in advance is up to you. It can be fifteen minutes or a few hours.)

1¼ pounds potatoes, 3 to 4 medium

1 medium onion

1 cup olive oil

Salt and freshly ground black pepper

6 extra-large or jumbo eggs

1 Peel and thinly slice the potatoes and onion; it's easiest if you use a mandoline for slicing. Meanwhile, heat the oil in an 8- or 10-inch skillet over medium heat. After the oil has been heating for 3 or 4 minutes, drop in a slice of potato. When tiny bubbles appear around the edges of the potato, the oil is ready; add all of the potatoes and onion along with a good pinch of salt and a liberal sprinkling of pepper. Gently turn the potato mixture in the oil with a wooden spoon, and adjust the heat so that the oil bubbles lazily.

2 Cook, turning the potatoes gently every few minutes and adjusting the heat so they do not brown, until they are tender when pierced with the point of a small knife. If the potatoes begin to break, they are overdone—this is not a tragedy, but stop the cooking immediately. As the potatoes cook, beat the eggs with some salt and pepper in a large bowl.

3 Drain the potatoes in a colander, reserving the oil. Heat an 8- or 9-inch nonstick skillet (it can be the same one, but wipe it out first) over medium heat for a minute and add 2 tablespoons of the reserved oil. Gently mix the warm potatoes with the eggs and add them to the skillet. As soon as the edges firm up—this will only take a

WINE Rioja or other soft, rich red.

SERVE WITH This is most frequently served as a tapa—snack—in Spain, but it's a great starter or main course, depending on quantity. With bread and a salad, it makes a complete meal.

minute or so—reduce the heat to medium-low. Cook 5 minutes.

4 Insert a rubber spatula all around the edges of the cake to make sure it will slide from the pan. Carefully slide it out—the top will still be quite runny—onto a plate. Cover with another plate and, holding the plates tightly, invert them. Add another tablespoon of oil to the skillet and use a rubber spatula to coax the cake back in. Cook another 5 minutes, then slide the cake from the skillet to a plate. (Alternatively, finish the cooking by putting the tortilla in a 350°F oven for about 10 minutes.) Serve warm (not hot) or at room temperature. Do not refrigerate.

A NONSTICK SKILLET is practically a must here.

THE POTATO AND ONION are cooked in lots of olive oil until soft but not at all crisp. Most of this olive oil is drained, and it should be reserved for other uses, especially sautéing and stir-frying.

IT'S IMPORTANT TO avoid browning the potatoes, which is easy enough, and to keep the omelet from overcooking—also not that difficult, as long as the heat is kept moderate and the cooking time relatively short.

THE ONLY HARD PART is turning the partially formed cake, but if you act swiftly and carefully you will succeed. The worst that will happen is that a couple of slices of

potato and a dribble of egg will be left behind when you return the cake to the skillet, but this will not affect the final product. (If the process makes you nervous, you can finish the tortilla in the oven; see the recipe.)

With MINIMAL Effort

Although potatoes are the most widely enjoyed filling, the tortilla is often filled with a variety of ingredients. Just make sure that any additions are either cooked in olive oil or thoroughly drained of other liquids.

- Replace the potatoes with greens cooked like the spinach on page 174 (start with about a pound). Squeeze the greens dry and chop them, then sauté in just a couple of tablespoons of olive oil before adding the eggs.

- Add about a cup of red bell pepper strips to the potatoes as they cook.

- Add ¼ cup or more of diced chorizo, cooked bacon or shrimp, or dry cured ham like prosciutto to the eggs.

- Add ½ cup or more of canned or cooked fresh peas, lima beans, or chickpeas to the eggs.

Sauces and Condiments

Parsley-Vinegar Sauce

TIME: 10 minutes

MAKES: 4 servings, about 1 cup

Parsley is the most underrated herb in the United States, but when you get past using parsley as a garnish and sprinkle a handful on top of a dish just before serving, you begin to appreciate the bright, clean flavor of this common herb. And when you realize that it remains in season for longer than basil, rosemary, or other popular herbs, you get a further sense of its value. You can also blend parsley with vinegar to make a sharp, spiky sauce that complements simply prepared, full-flavored foods. I first had this sauce (or something very much like it) with *bollito misto*, the Italian dish of assorted boiled meats.

1 cup packed parsley leaves (about 1 ounce), washed and dried

1 tablespoon extra virgin olive oil

1 small garlic clove, peeled

Salt and freshly ground black pepper

⅓ cup rice, sherry, or other good, fairly mild vinegar

1 Place the parsley in a food processor along with the oil, garlic, a healthy pinch of salt, and about ¼ teaspoon pepper. With the machine on, drizzle the vinegar through the feed tube until the parsley is pureed.

2 Add 1 tablespoon water and pulse the machine on and off a couple of times; taste. The mixture should be sharp, but not overpoweringly so. If it seems too strong, add a little more water (the texture will be quite loose, something like thick orange juice). Taste and add more salt and pepper if necessary. Pass the sauce at the table, using a spoon to serve it.

WINE Vinegar-based sauces kill good wine, so keep it simple and inexpensive; the type of wine will be determined by the food with which you serve the sauce.

SERVE WITH This is an ideal accompaniment to the simplest grilled, broiled, or roasted meat—great on well-browned steaks, pork, or chicken, or on Salmon Burgers (page 82).

ALTHOUGH MANY SOURCES insist that flat-leaf parsley is better than the curly-leaf variety, blind tastings have not borne out that myth. What matters more is freshness—limp parsley has less flavor.

PARSLEY MAY BE SANDY, so wash it well. In the quantity given here, it's worth using a salad spinner to dry it.

THE VINEGAR YOU USE should be mild and not too intensely flavored; a good rice or sherry vinegar, with an acidity level of about 6 percent, works best. Stronger vinegar should be diluted even more than indicated in the recipe.

- Increase the amount of olive oil to as much as ½ cup; eliminate the water (you can also eliminate the vinegar if you like, for a more pestolike dressing).

- Add toasted walnuts or pignolis, about 2 tablespoons, after the water. Pulse just until the nuts are chopped.

- Add the chopped white of a hard-cooked egg or two.

- Add grated Parmesan or other hard cheese to taste, at least 2 tablespoons.

- Substitute a shallot for the garlic.

Basic Vinaigrette: The Mother of All Dressings

TIME: 10 minutes

MAKES: About ⅔ cup

It's hard to imagine five minutes in the kitchen better spent than those making vinaigrette, the closest thing to an all-purpose sauce. At its most basic, vinaigrette is acid and oil, salt and pepper, plus additional flavors as desired. But behind this apparent simplicity lies a complex web of questions to be addressed: Which acid? Which oil? What else should be added? How should it all be combined?

Although the answers to all of these questions are subjective, there is a more-or-less standard vinaigrette that has evolved in the kitchens of many good cooks. It's simple, flexible, and, when made in a blender, so stable that it can be prepared hours before it is needed. Once made, it can be used on everything from a simple green salad to cold meat, vegetables, or fish dishes to anything that has been broiled or grilled, whether served hot or at room temperature.

½ cup extra virgin olive oil

3 tablespoons or more good wine vinegar

Salt and freshly ground black pepper

1 heaping teaspoon Dijon mustard

1 large shallot (about 1 ounce), peeled and cut into chunks

1 Combine all ingredients except the shallot in a blender and turn the machine on; a creamy emulsion will form within 30 seconds. Taste and add more vinegar, a teaspoon or two at a time, until the balance tastes right to you.

2 Add the shallot and turn the machine on and off a few times until the shallot is minced within the dressing. Taste and adjust seasoning and serve. (This is best made fresh but will keep, refrigerated, for a few days; bring back to room temperature and whisk briefly before using.)

WINE Like most vinegar-based sauces, vinaigrette is not especially wine-friendly. Keep it simple and inexpensive.

SERVE WITH Vinaigrette is the all-purpose dressing, useful almost anywhere. It's most common on salads, but is great on grilled food and steamed and simmered vegetables as well.

THE STANDARD RATIO for making vinaigrette is three parts oil to one part vinegar, but because the vinegars I use are mild and extra virgin olive oil is quite assertive, I usually wind up at about two parts oil to one part vinegar, or even a little stronger. Somewhere in that range you're going to find a home for your own taste; start by using a ratio of three to one and taste, adding more vinegar until you're happy. (You may even prefer more vinegar than olive oil; there's nothing wrong with that.)

TO VARY THE FLAVOR, try walnut or hazelnut oil or, if you want to downplay the flavor of oil altogether, a neutral oil such as grapeseed or canola.

USE GOOD WINE VINEGAR, preferably but not necessarily Champagne vinegar, or the extra-mild rice vinegar. (Balsamic and sherry vinegars, while delicious, are too dominant for some uses, fine for others.) Lemon juice is a fine substitute, but because it is less acidic than most vinegars—3 or 4 percent compared to 6 or 7 percent—you will need more of it.

THE INGREDIENTS MAY BE combined with a spoon, a fork, a whisk, or a blender. Hand tools give you an unconvincing emulsion that must be used immediately. Blenders produce vinaigrettes that very much resemble thin mayonnaise in color and thickness—without using egg. They also dispose of the job of mincing the shallots; just peel, chop, and dump it into the container at the last minute (if you add it earlier it will be pureed, depriving you of the pleasure of its distinctive crunch).

You can integrate almost anything that appeals to you into your vinaigrette. Some quick ideas, many of which may be combined:

- Any fresh or dried herb, fresh by the teaspoon or tablespoon, dried by the pinch

- Minced fresh garlic and/or ginger to taste

- Soy sauce, Worcestershire sauce, meat or vegetable stock, or other liquid seasonings, as much as 1 tablespoon

- Honey or other sweeteners to taste

- Whole-grain or dry mustard to taste

- Cayenne pepper or crushed red pepper flakes, minced fresh hot chiles, or grated or prepared horseradish to taste

- Freshly grated Parmesan or other hard cheese, or crumbled Roquefort or other blue cheese, at least 1 tablespoon

- Capers, or minced pickles, preferably cornichons, at least 1 tablespoon

- Sour cream, yogurt, or pureed soft tofu, about 2 tablespoons

- Ground spices, such as curry powder, five-spice powder, or nutmeg, in very small quantities

Reduction Sauce

Gravy, whether made from turkey or any other roasted meat or poultry, is just one of many possible variations on a basic reduction sauce. And reduction sauce is little more than a fancy term for degreasing (or, if you want to be nice, "deglazing") the pan.

When you roast or sauté meat or poultry at high heat, bits of skin, meat, and fat stick to the surface of the pan, becoming dark brown and concentrated; meat juices and rendered fat also gather at the bottom. If you remove the meat, add liquid to the pan, and place it over high heat while stirring, you incorporate these essences into that liquid. At the same time, some of the liquid you added evaporates—reduces—thereby intensifying its own flavor and thickening slightly.

Reduction sauces are easy, involve just a few basic steps, and can be doubled or tripled in size.

2 tablespoons minced shallot, onion, or scallion

3 cups stock or water

2 tablespoons olive oil or softened butter, optional

Salt and freshly ground black pepper

1 Remove the meat from the roasting pan or skillet and pour off all but 1 or 2 tablespoons of the cooking fat (if there are nonfatty juices in the skillet or roasting pan, leave them in there). Place the pan over high heat (use two burners if the pan is large). Add the shallot and cook, stirring, until it softens, about 1 minute.

2 Add the liquid and cook, stirring and scraping to loosen the brown bits at the bottom of the pan. Allow the liquid to boil for about 5 minutes, or until about a third of it evaporates. (This is a good time to carve the meat, if necessary, as the boiling liquid need not be stirred except very occasionally.)

3 Turn the heat to medium-low and add the optional butter or oil, a little at a time, stirring well after each addition to incorporate it. Taste and season if necessary with salt and pepper to taste, then serve with the meat.

WINE Reduction sauces can be quite elegant, so you may choose something really good; whether it's red or white depends on the center-of-the-plate food.

SERVE WITH Reduction sauces almost always begin with another preparation, so you're set for meat, poultry or fish. Usually, rice, bread, or potatoes are good side dishes, so you can mop up the plate.

STOCK IS THE MOST COMMON reduction liquid. In moderation, so are cream, milk, wine, fortified wine (like sherry or port), fruit or vegetable juice, or even the liquid used to soak dried mushrooms. But water is also perfectly acceptable, since the pan drippings contain plenty of flavor.

MOST REDUCTION SAUCES are finished with a bit of butter or oil to add creaminess and even more flavor. It's not essential, but it's good.

Thickened Gravy: Combine 1 tablespoon cornstarch with ¼ cup cold water (it will dissolve easily). Stir this into the sauce after incorporating the optional butter or oil and heat, stirring, until thickened, just about a minute. If you want even thicker gravy, repeat with another tablespoon of cornstarch.

■ Add 1 cup or more roughly chopped aromatic vegetables (carrots, onions, celery, etc.) to the roasting pan along with the meat, right from the beginning of cooking.

■ Increase the amount and kind of vegetables sautéed in the roasting fat. For example, add minced carrots and mushrooms along with the shallots. (You will probably want to strain the gravy if you do this; do so before adding butter or thickening, because it will pass through the strainer more easily; then reheat the sauce and enrich or thicken it as desired.)

■ Reduce ½ to 1 cup of wine, fortified wine (like sherry or port), or fruit or vegetable juice to just a couple of tablespoons before adding the stock or water.

■ Make the flavor even stronger by stirring in a teaspoon or more of prepared mustard, horseradish, soy sauce, or other condiment.

■ Add minced fresh or dried herbs to the mixture along with the shallot: a few tablespoons of parsley or small amounts of sage, tarragon, or thyme are all good. You can also add capers, anchovies, chopped bell pepper, or minced garlic.

■ Add bits of chopped meat to the sauce along with the shallot, or simply stir them into the finished sauce.

Sun-Dried Tomato Sauce

It's not widely known that you can make a simple pounded sauce from sun-dried tomatoes, but Fred Plotkin includes a sketchy but informative recipe for sun-dried tomato sauce in his inspiring *Recipes from Paradise*, a cookbook about Liguria, also known as the Italian Riviera. Mr. Plotkin is intentionally vague about the sauce's ingredients and their quantities, because he believes that everything beyond the distinct flavor of the dried tomato and the olive oil in which it soaks is nearly superfluous. With his guidance, and some experimentation, I've given the recipe a little more structure, but there remains plenty of latitude here in terms of quantities and additional ingredients.

½ cup softened sun-dried tomatoes (see Keys to Success), with their oil

1 small or ½ large garlic clove, or to taste

Salt

4 chopped basil leaves, optional

1 tablespoon fresh lemon juice, optional

3 tablespoons pignoli nuts

Additional extra virgin olive oil if necessary

1 Place the tomatoes and a tablespoon or so of their oil in a small food processor along with the garlic and a good pinch of salt. Process until fairly smooth, stopping the machine and stirring down the mixture with a rubber spatula as necessary.

2 Add the basil and lemon juice if you like; pulse the machine a few times to blend. Remove the paste from the machine and stir in, by hand, the nuts and just enough additional oil to make the mixture silky rather than oily. Taste and adjust seasoning. The sauce will keep, covered with a thin layer of oil and refrigerated in a tightly covered container, for at least a week. But its flavor is best when served immediately.

WINE Nothing too soft—a crisp white or fruity, bright red.

SERVE WITH This sauce is going to be the dominant flavor in almost any meal in which it is included; keep everything else simple.

YOU CAN BUY SUN-DRIED tomatoes already reconstituted and soaked in olive oil, but they're expensive. It's certainly easy enough—and only slightly less convenient if you think ahead—to begin with dried tomatoes. They're as tough as shoe leather when you buy them, but can be easily reconstituted: Soak them in hot water to cover until they're soft, about an hour. (You might change the water once it cools to hasten the softening.) Drain the tomatoes and marinate them in a good, light, fruity olive oil to cover (one-half cup or more) for at least an hour.

AFTER THAT, making the tomato paste takes just a moment. Traditionally, the tomatoes are pounded, usually with garlic, in a mortar and pestle. I use a small food processor and like the resulting texture very much. Mr. Plotkin adds a little lemon juice to the mixture as well as some pignoli nuts, and I think a touch of basil really brings the sauce to life.

Some of the many uses for this sauce:

■ As a pasta sauce, but sparingly, and thinned with a little of the hot pasta-cooking water

■ As a spread on bread or sandwiches

■ As a dip for raw vegetables or crackers

■ As a condiment for chicken or fish

■ As a sauce for cooked bland vegetables, such as boiled potatoes

Mayonnaise

TIME: 10 minutes

MAKES: 1 cup

Whether you work by hand or with a blender or food processor, it takes just five minutes to make mayonnaise, and when you're done you have a flavorful, creamy dressing that is so far superior to the bottled stuff you may not recognize it as the same thing. Next to vinaigrette, it's the most useful of all dressings, and despite its luxurious nature, it contains little saturated fat.

1 egg or egg yolk
2 teaspoons Dijon mustard
Salt and freshly ground black pepper

1 cup olive or other oil
1 tablespoon freshly squeezed lemon juice or vinegar

1 To make the mayonnaise by hand: Combine the egg, mustard, and salt and pepper to taste in a medium bowl. Use a wire whisk to combine, then add the oil in a thin, steady stream, beating all the while. When the mixture becomes thick and creamy, you can add the oil a little faster. When it is all integrated, whisk in the lemon juice. Taste and adjust seasoning.

To make the mayonnaise in a blender or food processor: Combine the egg, mustard, and salt and pepper in the machine's container and pulse on and off a few times. With the machine running, add the oil, slowly, through the top or feed tube. When the mixture becomes thick and creamy, you can add the oil a little faster. When it is all integrated, pulse in the lemon juice. Taste and adjust seasoning.

2 If the mayonnaise is thicker than you like (a distinct possibility if you're using a machine), thin with warm water, sweet cream, or sour cream.

WINE Determined by the center-of-the-plate food. Mayonnaise is quite wine-friendly.

SERVE WITH Works wonders with cold cooked meats or fish, salads, raw vegetables, you name it; essential in Turkey Tonnato, page 126.

MAYONNAISE IS BEST made with yolks for best color and flavor; you can use a whole egg if you prefer.

OLIVE OIL MAKES a great mayonnaise, but so do neutral oils like canola and grapeseed. (Make sure the oil is fresh, because this is an oil-dominated, uncooked sauce, and you'll notice any off flavors.)

I GENERALLY USE LEMON JUICE, but vinegar is just as good, and the quantity is so small it hardly makes a difference.

- If you're worried about the health aspects of using a raw egg, start with bottled mayonnaise and beat in a little oil and/or any of the suggested additions.

 Like vinaigrette, the flavor of mayonnaise can be almost infinitely varied. Many of the suggested ingredients can be combined; use your judgment.

- Add a clove of peeled garlic at the beginning. Try adding ½ cup roasted red peppers (or canned pimiento) and a little cayenne pepper at the same time.

- Vary the kind of acid you use: lime or orange juice, or any type of vinegar. If the acidity is too strong when you're done, beat in a little warm water.

- Add 2 or 3 anchovy fillets at the beginning.

- Add any fresh herbs you like. Start with a small amount and taste, adding more at the end if you like. If you're using a machine, they will turn the mayonnaise green. If you're working by hand, you will have herb-flecked mayonnaise.

- Add horseradish, Worcestershire sauce, or spices or spice mixes to the finished mayonnaise, tasting as you go.

Cumin-Tomato Relish and Pan-Grilled Tomato Salsa

TIME: 10 minutes

MAKES: 4 to 6 servings

Here are two ideas for what to do with all those tomatoes that begin appearing in July and August. The first is uncooked—chopped tomatoes combined with seasonings. I add onion, red bell pepper, and some cumin seeds for crunch. The second, Pan-Grilled Tomato Salsa, is a charred tomato dish that's the type of thing you have in restaurants, but it is easy enough to make at home. The blackened tomatoes are combined with just enough oil and vinegar to make the whole thing juicy.

Cumin-Tomato Salsa

2 teaspoons cumin seeds or ground cumin

1½ pounds plum or other tomatoes, cored and roughly chopped

½ red bell pepper, seeded, stemmed, and minced, optional

1 tablespoon minced onion

Salt and cayenne pepper

Juice of 1 lime

2 tablespoons chopped cilantro

1 If you're using cumin seeds, place them in a small skillet and toast over medium heat, shaking the pan occasionally, until they are fragrant, just a minute or two. Finely grind all but ½ teaspoon.

2 Combine the tomatoes, optional bell pepper, onion, salt, cayenne, ground cumin, and lime juice; taste and adjust seasoning if necessary. Just before serving, toss with the cilantro and reserved whole cumin seeds. (This can be refrigerated for up to a day or two; bring to room temperature before serving.)

WINE Both of these go well with the kind of food that goes well with light red wines, like Zinfandel and Beaujolais.

SERVE WITH Serve the relish with grilled meats; it's also great on hamburgers (or with Salmon Burgers, page 82) and sandwiches. The salsa is a fine accompaniment to grilled fish or chicken; it also can serve as a side dish.

Pan-Grilled Tomato Salsa

3 large, meaty tomatoes, cored
and cut into thick slices

¼ cup extra virgin olive oil

2 tablespoons sherry or balsamic vinegar

Salt and freshly ground black
pepper

1 Heat a large skillet, preferably cast iron or nonstick, over medium-high heat for about 5 minutes. Add the tomatoes, raise the heat to high, and cook until lightly charred on one side, 3 to 5 minutes. Turn and cook the other side very lightly, about 1 minute. If necessary, work in batches to avoid crowding the tomatoes.

2 Combine the olive oil and vinegar in a large, shallow dish and, as the tomatoes are done, turn them in the mixture. Season and serve as a side dish, or as a sauce for grilled or roasted fish or chicken. (This can be refrigerated for up to a day or two; bring to room temperature before serving.)

With MINIMAL Effort

■ The relish is good with chili powder in place of cumin, and, if you like hot food, great with a bit of minced jalapeño or habenero chile.

■ The salsa is wonderful with added herbs, especially basil.

Keys To SUCCESS

NEITHER OF THESE RECIPES requires peeling the tomatoes, but they should be cored: Use a paring knife to cut a cone-shaped wedge out of the stem end and remove it.

Rosemary-Lemon White Bean Dip

TIME: 10 minutes (with precooked or canned beans)

MAKES: 8 servings

This wonderful bean dip originally came to me from Lidia Bastianich, one of the great Italian educators, chefs, and TV personalities. It has more life than most dips but does without the harshness of raw garlic usually associated with Middle Eastern hummus or Southwestern purees. Still, it's pretty simple, with the not-exactly-exotic "mystery" ingredient of grated lemon zest, which is quite substantial in both quantity and size of the pieces.

2 cups cooked cannellini or other white beans, drained but quite moist

1 to 3 garlic cloves, peeled

Salt and freshly ground black pepper

¼ cup plus 1 tablespoon extra virgin olive oil

2 teaspoons minced fresh rosemary

Grated zest of 2 lemons

1 Put the beans in the container of a food processor with 1 garlic clove and a healthy pinch of salt. Turn the machine on and add the ¼ cup olive oil in a steady stream through the feed tube; process until the mixture is smooth. Taste and add more garlic if you like, then puree again.

2 Place the mixture in a bowl and use a wooden spoon to beat in the rosemary, lemon zest, and remaining 1 tablespoon olive oil. Taste and add salt and pepper as needed. Use immediately or refrigerate up to 3 days.

WINE Will depend on the center-of-the-plate food.

SERVE WITH Use the puree as a dip for breadsticks, pita or other bread, or raw vegetables. Or combine a thick layer of puree with grilled vegetables and a little olive oil on rolls or between thick slices of crusty bread. A small mound of the puree served next to some braised escarole or other bitter greens, both drizzled with olive oil, makes a fine side dish. Serve it at the center of a plate of lightly and simply cooked vegetables—carrots, green beans, turnips, asparagus, potatoes, cauliflower, and so on.

LIKE MOST BEAN DISHES, this puree is best if you use freshly cooked dried beans, but it is still good with canned beans. One-half pound of dried beans will yield about two cups, the amount needed for this recipe, although you can double the quantities if you like.

IF YOU USE DRIED BEANS, cook them in unsalted water to cover (presoaking is unnecessary), with a couple of bay leaves, until very tender. (Cooked beans can be frozen quite successfully in their cooking water.)

IF YOU USE CANNED BEANS, you'll need almost two full fifteen-ounce cans to get two cups (there's a lot of water in those cans).

■ Thyme or basil instead of rosemary is terrific, or use shallots in place of garlic for a milder flavor.

■ Replace the lemon with orange.

■ The puree can be used to thicken and flavor cooked beans. Just stir a few spoonfuls of the puree into simmering white beans (if you have pesto, add some at the same time). Thinned with bean- or pasta-cooking water, this makes a good pasta sauce.

Fig Relish

Like chestnuts, fresh figs are so common in Mediterranean countries that they are taken for granted, but here (outside of California at least) they are still pretty exotic. Still, these days you can find fresh figs not only at pricey gourmet markets but at farm stands and Italian grocery stores everywhere, and even at many supermarkets. While the best way to eat figs is out of hand—few fruits are as luxurious tasting—there are rewarding ways to use them in recipes; here's one of them.

8 ounces fresh figs

1 tablespoon minced capers

Zest of 1 lemon, minced

Juice of 1 lemon

2 tablespoons olive oil

Salt and freshly ground black pepper

2 tablespoons chopped parsley

2 tablespoons chopped basil, optional

1 Gently rinse and stem the figs; chop them into about ¼-inch pieces, making sure to catch all of their juices. Toss in a bowl with the capers, lemon zest and juice, olive oil, and salt and pepper to taste. Just before serving (you can wait up to two hours), add the herbs, then taste and adjust the seasonings.

WINE It will depend on the food you're serving it with, but most likely you'll be wanting a red with some substance.

SERVE WITH The fig relish is especially brilliant on grilled swordfish or tuna (try it on Grilled Fish the Mediterranean Way, page 74), but nearly as good with grilled or broiled chicken (especially dark meat), pork, lamb, or beef. (Note that all of these foods contain some fat; because the relish is so lean, combining it with non-fatty meats or fish—such as boneless chicken or flounder—produces a dish that seems to lack substance.)

Keys To SUCCESS

YOU CAN USE PURPLE or green figs for this, but either should be ripe enough to eat.

THE TRICKIEST PART of this recipe is balancing sweetness and acidity, which can only be done by using your taste and your judgment.

With MINIMAL Effort

■ Add a tiny amount (¼ teaspoon or so) of minced garlic. Alternatively, crush a garlic clove and let it sit in the mixture for a few minutes, then fish it out just before serving.

■ Add a teaspoon or more of minced shallot.

■ Add a couple of teaspoons of chopped olives or anchovies.

■ Substitute lime zest and juice or mild vinegar for the lemon.

■ Change the herbs; a teaspoon of minced thyme or rosemary in place of the basil makes the relish considerably more pungent.

Dried Mushroom Puree

It isn't often that you can make a condiment with a single dried ingredient, but since dried mushrooms have become widely available, that is exactly what has happened. If you simmer dried mushrooms until tender, then toss them in a blender with their cooking liquid, you get a thick puree, potent and delicious.

The result is very much like the classic duxelles, in which fresh mushrooms and their scraps are cooked only until their essence remains. But this procedure requires almost no preparation: no cleaning, no chopping, and hardly any cooking, because the mushrooms have already been dried and there is no need to cook out their water.

1 ounce dried porcini mushrooms (about ½ cup, loosely packed)

Salt and freshly ground black pepper

1 Combine the mushrooms with 2½ cups water in a 4- or 6-cup saucepan and turn the heat to medium-high. Bring to a boil, then adjust the heat so the mixture simmers gently. Cook until the mushrooms are tender, about 15 minutes.

2 Remove the mushrooms with a slotted spoon and place in the container of a blender. Strain the liquid through a paper towel in a sieve, or through a couple of layers of cheesecloth; there will be about 1 cup. Add most of the liquid to the mushrooms and puree, adding the remaining liquid if necessary to allow the machine to do its work.

3 Season to taste with salt and pepper and serve, or cover and refrigerate for up to a couple of days.

WINE Most likely red, to be determined by the center-of-the-plate food.

SERVE WITH Stir the puree into risotto or other grain preparations (be sure to use any of the leftover mushroom-cooking liquid in cooking the grain); include it in omelets or in pizzas; thin it with butter or olive oil to make a sauce for meat or fish; or simply use it as you would ketchup.

YOU CAN USE ANY dried mushrooms for this condiment, from the extremely inexpensive shiitakes (also called black mushrooms) sold in Asian markets to the prince of dried mushrooms, the porcini. Smoky porcini (usually imported from Chile or Poland) are really good here.

The sauce can be made more complex by the addition of seasonings beyond salt and pepper, and the process is easy. When pureeing the mushrooms, add:

- A peeled shallot or small garlic clove

- A teaspoon of thyme leaves (or ½ teaspoon dried thyme)

- A tablespoon of Port, tomato paste, or soy sauce

In each case, be sure to taste the puree before you remove it from the blender; the mushroom flavor is so strong that it may take a relatively large quantity of complementary seasoning to make its presence felt.

Red Pepper Puree

Roasted red pepper puree is more useful than ketchup, simpler in composition, and far more delicious—you can eat it with a spoon. It contains two basic ingredients, red bell peppers and olive oil, and both are always readily available. And since making a batch is about as difficult as scrambling an egg, and the puree stores fairly well, there's little reason not to have some on hand.

4 large red bell peppers, about 2 pounds

Salt

½ cup extra virgin olive oil

1 Preheat the oven to 500°F. Line a roasting pan with enough aluminum foil to fold over the top later. Place the bell peppers in the pan and the pan in the oven. Roast, turning the peppers about every 10 minutes, until they collapse, about 40 minutes.

2 Fold the foil over the peppers and allow them to cool. Working over a bowl, remove the core, skin, and seeds from each of the peppers, reserving some of the liquid.

3 Place the pepper pulp in the container of a food processor with about 2 tablespoons of the reserved liquid. Add a large pinch of salt and turn on the machine; drizzle the oil in through the feed tube. Stop the machine, then taste and add more salt and/or olive oil if necessary. Store, well covered, in the refrigerator (for several days) or the freezer (up to a month).

WINE Will be entirely determined by the center-of-the-plate food; could be white or red.

SERVE WITH See With Minimal Effort.

THE BEST METHOD FOR roasting peppers uses the oven. You can skip this step entirely by beginning with canned or bottled pimientos, which are roasted peppers packed with natural or chemical preservatives. Their flavor, however, is relatively flat.

ONCE THE PEPPERS ARE ROASTED and peeled, pureeing them takes just a minute in a food processor.

■ Add a couple of tablespoons of puree to the cooking liquid of any simmering grain—rice, couscous, or quinoa, for example. The color is glorious.

■ Use in place of or with tomatoes in pasta sauce. For example, sauté several vegetables and bind them with the puree during the last minute of cooking.

■ Fold into omelets or scrambled eggs, with or without cooked vegetables.

■ Combine with chopped basil, grated Parmesan, and minced garlic for a pestolike pasta sauce.

■ Emulsify with fresh lemon juice, salt, and pepper to make a beautiful salad dressing.

■ Spread on crostini, bruschetta, or pizza before baking.

■ Use as a finishing sauce for roasted eggplant, zucchini, or other vegetables.

■ Serve as a condiment with grilled or roasted fish, meat, or chicken.

■ Stir into soups or stews just before serving.

■ Mash a couple of tablespoons of puree, with a little olive oil, minced garlic, and cracked black pepper, into fresh, salty cheese—such as feta or goat—to make a dip for bread or vegetables.

■ Flavor the puree with any number of herbs (thyme, basil, and parsley are fine) or spices, like cumin or chili powder (or minced chiles).

Desserts

Strawberries with Balsamic Vinegar

TIME: 15 minutes
MAKES: 4 to 6 servings

Here's a strawberry dessert that is not only delicious and intriguing, but can compete with plain fruit in lightness. Strawberries are sugared to juice them up a bit, then drizzled with balsamic vinegar, and sprinkled with a pinch of black pepper. The result is so elegant that you'll find it in great restaurants from here to Emilia-Romagna, the home of balsamic vinegar.

1 quart strawberries, rinsed, hulled, and sliced, or a mixture of strawberries, blueberries, and blackberries

¼ cup sugar, or more to taste

1 teaspoon high-quality balsamic vinegar, or more to taste

About ⅛ teaspoon freshly ground black pepper

1 Toss the strawberries and optional blueberries or blackberries with ¼ cup sugar and let sit for 10 minutes or longer. (Do not refrigerate.)

2 Sprinkle with vinegar; toss gently, then taste and add more sugar or vinegar if necessary. Sprinkle with the pepper, toss again, and serve.

WINE Slightly sweet, lightly sparkling wine, such as Muscat.

SERVE WITH This is an ideal dessert after a heavy meal. Serve, if you like, with a few crisp cookies, or a slice of pound, sponge, or angel food cake.

IDEALLY, YOU'LL MAKE THIS dessert with ripe, local berries and authentic balsamic vinegar, which is expensive but used in tiny quantities, as it is here.

STRAWBERRIES WITH BALSAMIC vinegar will not hold for any length of time. You can sugar the berries an hour or two before you want to serve them, but no longer.

■ Garnish with chopped fresh mint leaves.

Grilled Fruit Skewers
with Ginger Syrup

TIME: 30 minutes
MAKES: 4 servings

This dish, a mélange of quickly grilled fruit brushed with a ginger sauce that itself takes about five minutes to put together, was created by my friend Johnny Earles. The sauce is a simple sugar syrup—equal parts of sugar and water, boiled together until the sugar melts—and then infused with a lot of ginger.

½ cup sugar

½ cup water

¼ cup thinly sliced fresh ginger (don't bother to peel it)

4 bananas, not overly ripe

1 small pineapple

1 carambola, optional

1 Start a gas or charcoal fire; the fire should be quite hot, and the rack positioned 4 to 6 inches from the heat source. Combine the first three ingredients in a saucepan over medium heat. Bring to a boil and simmer for 3 minutes. Remove from the heat and let sit while you prepare the fruit.

2 Do not peel the bananas; cut them into 2-inch-long chunks and make a shallow vertical slit in the skin to facilitate peeling at the table. Peel and core the pineapple, then cut it into 2-inch chunks. Cut the carambola, if you're using it, into ½-inch-thick slices.

3 Skewer the fruit. Strain the syrup and brush the fruit lightly with it. Grill the fruit until the pineapple is nicely browned, 2 to 4 minutes per side. As it is grilling, brush occasionally with the syrup.

4 When the fruit is done, brush once more with syrup; serve hot or warm.

WINE Light, slightly sweet, and preferably sparkling.
SERVE WITH A nice dessert at any grilled meal.

WHATEVER FUEL YOU use here, make sure the fire is hot, and keep the grilling time short.

MANY FRUITS CAN BE GRILLED, but pineapple browns beautifully and banana develops a luxurious creaminess; carambola, also called starfruit, is another good selection, although not always easy to find.

SUGAR SYRUP KEEPS for weeks, refrigerated, and is the sweetener of choice for iced tea.

■ Use other flavors in place of the ginger: mint, lemon verbena, thyme, even chile.

Dried Fruit Poached in Port

Nothing can match dried fruit for convenience and intensity of flavor. And when you poach an assortment with Port and a few spices, the results belie the ease of preparation. This is not a summer dessert—no one would mistake this for fresh fruit—but it is delicious, low-fat, and a welcome change from heavy winter desserts.

12 prunes	5 allspice berries
8 dried figs	5 peppercorns
4 dried apricot or peach halves	1 star anise
4 dried pear halves	1-inch cinnamon stick
3 pieces candied ginger	1 cup Port
1 clove	

1 Combine all ingredients in a medium saucepan and bring to a boil. Turn heat to very low and cover. Cook about 30 minutes, at which point most of the port will have been absorbed.

2 If the fruit is tender, it's done. If not, add ½ cup water, bring to a boil again, cover, and cook another 15 minutes. Repeat once more if necessary.

3 Remove the fruit with a slotted spoon, then strain the liquid to remove the spices. Serve a portion of the fruit warm, cold, or at room temperature with a spoonful or two of its juice.

WINE What else? Port.
SERVE WITH Serve with a bit of sweet or sour cream, yogurt, or crème fraîche.

SINCE THE PREPARATION of this dish is absolutely fool-proof, the challenge lies entirely in the shopping, and one of the great things about dried fruit is that organic specimens are readily available; another is the incredible variety of fruits now being dried. In the course of fine-tuning this recipe, I tried not only the obvious prunes, figs, apricots, peaches, and pears, but cherries, blueberries, strawberries, pineapple, and even banana. I tend toward the traditional, but really enjoyed the tartness that dried pineapple added to the mixture; suit yourself.

USE A PORT YOU'LL ENJOY drinking, because you're going to use less than a third of the bottle in this recipe.

■ Substitute almost any sweet or neutral liquid for the Port: water, Oloroso sherry, red wine (add a tablespoon of sugar), sweet white wine, orange juice, and so on.

■ If you prefer less-than-sweet results, add a squeeze of fresh lemon juice at the end of cooking.

■ Vary the spices. Try a tiny grating of nutmeg in place of the allspice, peppercorns, and anise, for example. Some coriander seeds are also nice.

Fifteen-Minute Fruit Gratin

TIME: 15 minutes
MAKES: 4 servings

If you take soft, ripe fruit, top it with a fancy sauce like crème Anglaise, and run the whole thing under the broiler, you have a four-star dessert. But if you top the fruit with something like sweetened heavy cream, whipped just enough so that it holds some body when broiled, or sweetened sour cream—which hardly needs to be whisked—you can produce a similarly glorious dessert in less than half the time.

1 to 1½ pounds perfectly ripe, soft fruit, such as peaches and/or berries

1 cup heavy cream

3 tablespoons sugar

1 teaspoon vanilla extract

1 Preheat the broiler; set the rack as close to the heat source as possible (even 2 inches is not too close).

2 Wash, pit, stem, and peel the fruit as necessary. Cut stone fruit in halves or slices as you prefer. Cut strawberries in thick slices; leave smaller berries whole. Place the fruit—there should be at least 2 cups—in a baking or gratin dish just large enough to hold it.

3 Whip the cream with 2 tablespoons of the sugar and the vanilla until it is thick and just barely holding soft peaks. Pour it over and around the fruit. Sprinkle with the remaining 1 tablespoon sugar.

4 Broil carefully, allowing the cream to brown all over and even burn in a couple of spots; rotate the baking dish during broiling if necessary. Remove and serve.

WINE Can be lightly sweet, or intensely so.
SERVE WITH A few cookies are nice, but unnecessary.

THE TOPPINGS PRODUCE strikingly different results. Sour cream is thick, rich, flavorful, and (obviously) sour; sweet cream becomes thinner and saucier in texture. It also browns beautifully, and—especially if you begin with really good cream, that which hasn't been ultra-pasteurized—has a fresh subtlety that cannot be matched. I like both.

BE SURE THAT THE FRUIT you use is perfectly ripe. You're going to serve this dish with spoons, and the last thing you want is to have to reach for a knife and fork.

ALTHOUGH THIS PREPARATION is lightning-quick, it has to be constantly watched while cooking. Get the broiler hot, place the dish right under the heating element, and keep your eyes open. You want the topping to burn a little bit—it will smell like toasting marshmallows—but obviously not too much. When the topping is nearly uniformly brown, with a few black spots, it's done. The fruit will not have cooked at all.

Gratin with Sour Cream: Combine 1 cup sour cream with just enough milk—about ¼ cup—to allow you to whisk it smooth. Add 2 tablespoons sugar and proceed as above, using 1 tablespoon brown sugar for the topping.

■ Use figs, pitted prune plums, strawberries, raspberries, blueberries, peaches, alone or in combination.

One Batter, Many Cookies

TIME: 30 minutes
MAKES: About 4 dozen

Cookies are always easy to make, but even they can use streamlining. One solution is to whip up a single batter in a food processor and finish it in different ways. (You might call this "the mother of all butter cookies.") With this one dough you can flavor some, roll some, bake them at different temperatures, and fill a cookie plate with variety in no time.

1½ cups all-purpose flour
½ cup cornstarch
¾ cup sugar
Pinch salt

2 sticks chilled butter, cut into bits
1 teaspoon vanilla extract
1 egg
½ cup milk, more or less

1 Preheat the oven to 375°F.

2 Combine the flour, cornstarch, sugar, and salt in a food processor and pulse once or twice. Add the butter and pulse 10 or 20 times until the butter and flour are well combined. Add the vanilla and the egg and pulse 3 or 4 times. Add about half the milk and pulse 2 or 3 times. Add the remaining milk a little at a time, pulsing once or twice after each addition, until the dough holds together in a sticky mass.

3 Remove the dough from the machine to one or more bowls. Make cookies as described in Step 4, or make any of the cookies listed in With Minimal Effort.

4 Drop rounded teaspoons of dough (you can make the cookies larger or smaller if you like) onto a nonstick baking sheet, a sheet lined with parchment paper, or a lightly buttered baking sheet. If you want flat cookies, press the balls down with your fingers or the back of a spatula or wooden spoon. Bake 10 to 12 minutes, or until the cookies are done as you like them. Cool on a rack, then store, if necessary, in a covered container.

WINE Coffee or tea would be better.
SERVE WITH Ice cream, if you must.

THIS BASIC BATTER, which is great plain (with white sugar or brown, or even molasses), can be easily varied. With one batch of batter you can make four different types of cookies—add lemon juice and zest to one-fourth of it, for example, chopped walnuts to the second, raisins to the third, and coconut to the fourth. Finally, it can produce rolled-out, cut, and decorated cookies; just chill it first to make it easier to handle.

I'VE REFINED THE CLASSIC recipe to do all the mixing in the food processor, which is fast and easy. It's important to process the ingredients gently, letting the machine run no longer than necessary at each stage so as not to toughen the batter. You can, of course, make this batter in a standing mixer, or by hand. In either case, cream together the butter and sugar first, then add the mixed dry ingredients.

THE BAKING PROCEDURE is determined by the results you prefer. At 375°F, the edges brown nicely and the center of each cookie remains pale and tender after about eleven minutes of baking; at 350°F, there will be no browning and the cookies will take a minute or two longer. In either case, slightly longer baking times will produce crisp cookies. These times assume, of course, that your oven is reasonably accurate; since most ovens are not, check the cookies every minute or so after eight minutes have passed. Note that the timing of the first batch and subsequent batches will require less attention.

Butterscotch Cookies: Substitute half or more brown sugar for the white sugar, or simply add 1 tablespoon molasses along with the egg.

Citrus Cookies: Do not use the vanilla; add 1 tablespoon lemon juice and 2 teaspoons grated lemon or orange zest along with the egg.

Chocolate Chip Cookies: Stir about 1 cup of chocolate chips into the finished batter. (The butterscotch batter variation is good here.)

Chunky Cookies: To the finished batter, add about a cup of M&M's (or other similar candy), or roughly chopped walnuts, pecans, or cashews; slivered almonds; raisins; coconut; dried cherries.

Ginger Cookies: Add 1 tablespoon ground ginger to the dry ingredients. For even better flavor, add ¼ cup minced crystallized ginger to the batter by hand (this works well in addition to or in place of the ground ginger).

Spice Cookies: Add 1 teaspoon ground cinnamon, ¼ teaspoon each ground allspice and ground ginger, and 1 pinch each ground cloves and nutmeg to the dry ingredients.

Rolled Cookies: Freeze the dough batter for 15 minutes or refrigerate it for about 1 hour (or longer). Work half the batter at a time, and roll it on a lightly floured surface; it will absorb some flour at first but will soon become less sticky. Do not add more flour than necessary.

Roll about ¼ inch thick and cut with any cookie cutters; decorate as you like. Reduce the cooking time to 8 to 10 minutes.

Puffy Cookies: The basic cookies are flat. For airier cookies, add ½ teaspoon baking powder to the dry ingredients.

Index